Kennedy

A Captivating Guide to the Life of John F. Kennedy and Jacqueline Lee Kennedy Onassis

© Copyright 2017

All rights Reserved. No part of this book may be reproduced in any form without permission in writing from the author. Reviewers may quote brief passages in reviews.

Disclaimer: No part of this publication may be reproduced or transmitted in any form or by any means, mechanical or electronic, including photocopying or recording, or by any information storage and retrieval system, or transmitted by email without permission in writing from the publisher.

While all attempts have been made to verify the information provided in this publication, neither the author nor the publisher assumes any responsibility for errors, omissions or contrary interpretations of the subject matter herein.

This book is for entertainment purposes only. The views expressed are those of the author alone, and should not be taken as expert instruction or commands. The reader is responsible for his or her own actions.

Adherence to all applicable laws and regulations, including international, federal, state and local laws governing professional licensing, business practices, advertising and all other aspects of doing business in the US, Canada, UK or any other jurisdiction is the sole responsibility of the purchaser or reader.

Neither the author nor the publisher assumes any responsibility or liability whatsoever on behalf of the purchaser or reader of these materials. Any perceived slight of any individual or organization is purely unintentional.

Contents

INTRODUCTION TO JOHN F. KENNEDY AND JACQUELINE KENNEDY ONASSIS..1
    PART 1: JOHN F. KENNEDY..8
    A CAPTIVATING GUIDE TO THE LIFE OF JFK................................8

INTRODUCTION 9

CHAPTER ONE: CHILDHOOD AND EDUCATION.................12

CHAPTER TWO: PERSONAL LIFE..17

CHAPTER THREE: RELATIONSHIP WITH JACKIE KENNEDY...........22

CHAPTER FOUR: NAVAL SERVICE...24

CHAPTER FIVE: CONGRESSIONAL CAREER...........................27

CHAPTER SIX: 1960 PRESIDENTIAL RACE..............................30

CHAPTER SEVEN: PRESIDENCY—FOREIGN POLICY...........33

CHAPTER EIGHT: DOMESTIC POLICY......................................46

CHAPTER NINE: ASSASSINATION..57

CHAPTER TEN: LEGACY..60
    PART 2: JACKIE KENNEDY...62
    A CAPTIVATING GUIDE TO THE LIFE OF JACQUELINE KENNEDY ONASSIS 62

INTRODUCTION 63

CHAPTER ONE: CHILDHOOD AND EARLY EDUCATION 66
CHAPTER TWO: COLLEGE AND EARLY CAREER 73
CHAPTER THREE: RELATIONSHIP WITH JOHN F. KENNEDY 78
CHAPTER FOUR: MOTHERHOOD 82
CHAPTER FIVE: CAMPAIGN FOR PRESIDENCY 88
CHAPTER SIX: FIRST LADY 90
CHAPTER SEVEN: KENNEDY ASSASSINATION 97
CHAPTER EIGHT: LIFE FOLLOWING THE ASSASSINATION 101
CHAPTER NINE: COMING TO AN END 105
CHAPTER TEN: ONGOING ICONIC FIGURE 110
    PREVIEW OF WORLD WAR 2 115
    A CAPTIVATING GUIDE FROM BEGINNING TO END 115
    PREVIEW OF WINSTON CHURCHILL: 120
    A CAPTIVATING GUIDE TO THE LIFE OF WINSTON S. CHURCHILL 120
    PREVIEW OF FRANKLIN ROOSEVELT: 132
    A CAPTIVATING GUIDE TO THE LIFE OF FDR 132

Free Bonus from Captivating History (Available for a Limited time)

Hi History Lovers!

Now you have a chance to join our exclusive history list so you can get your first history ebook for free as well as discounts and a potential to get more history books for free! Simply visit the link below to join.

Captivatinghistory.com/ebook

Also, make sure to follow us on:

Twitter: @Captivhistory

Facebook: Captivating History: @captivatinghistory

Introduction to John F. Kennedy and Jacqueline Kennedy Onassis

Without a doubt, President John F. Kennedy and First Lady Jacqueline Kennedy took the White House by storm, holding court in an unprecedented fashion for an American presidency. No other presidential couple held quite the power, esteem, and reputation as they did—at least not in the memory of the American people. Their faces—both together and apart—appeared on magazine covers, in newspaper articles, on television, and printed on radio advertisements. Everyone in America knew their names and faces. From the First Lady's stylistic choices to the President's youth, from their Catholic roots to suspected dalliances, the Kennedy family's life was an open book. Everyone knew their story and to this day, people are fascinated by the impact the First Family had on America's past, present, and future.

Perhaps what springs to mind about Jack and Jackie are the rumors of infidelity or the spectacle of the president's assassination, which easily overtake the contributions they made individually. President John F. Kennedy in his capacity as a leader is remembered for both his domestic and foreign policy plans, which include his participation in the Bay of Pigs Invasion, the never-ending and seemingly impossible Race to Space with Russia, and his ideas for the "New Frontier" plan that landed him in the country's most esteemed office. Jacqueline Kennedy Onassis was herself an icon of beauty, grace, and charm. Her impenetrable style as the First Lady and her restoration of the White House garnered much attention as she smiled in front of the camera and moved gracefully in every public space. Together, President John F. Kennedy and First Lady Jacqueline Kennedy Onassis were a commanding force, but like all power couples, they struggled behind closed doors.

Over time, ideas about the Kennedy family's dynamics have altered. In earlier scholarship, historians studied how they worked alongside one another in tandem to create a smooth and efficient White House. Jacqueline Kennedy Onassis accompanied John F. Kennedy on political trips, planned events for the White House, and provided a great amount of support. While all that remains true, scholars now dig deeper to determine how the intricacies of their relationship actually worked. As the years pass, more and more people who witnessed the powerhouse marriage have different testimonies. Rumors of affairs solidified as truth, rampant depression and intense health issues surfaced, and what seemed like a well-structured family unit and political power team began to crumble, creating a more realistic vision of what it was like to live in the Kennedy household.

First of all, one must consider John F. Kennedy's solicitous sex life. While married to Jacqueline Kennedy Onassis, John F. Kennedy was reported to have had extramarital affairs with women that range from celebrities to White House employees. Some names include Marilyn Monroe, Gunilla von Post, Judith Campbell, Mary Pinchot Meyer, Marlene Dietrich, Mimi Alford, and—probably the most unfounded and improper relationship—Kennedy Onassis' personal secretary,

Pamela Turnure. In fact, reports say that President Kennedy kept a specific apartment suite for the sole purpose of privately meeting his many companions outside of the media's watching eyes. During his time in office, the affairs remained low on the scale of media attention, though, due to an accepted gentlemen's agreement of the time that such affairs were beyond the purview of the press. All the Secret Service agents were, of course, privy to the comings and goings of John F. Kennedy's suitors after he became President of the United States. It is thought that Kennedy Onassis had a few affairs of her own, though none so overt as President Kennedy's dalliances. Maybe this lack of media attention was due to the imposing worries surrounding foreign affairs, maybe it was the media's lack of trying to pursue this specific thread of news, or maybe John F. Kennedy just got lucky and had a lot of people in the White House who kept their lips sealed. Regardless of the reason, the affairs remained relatively low-key in light of other American issues.

There is a possibility that Jacqueline Kennedy Onassis' pure and unadulterated hatred for the media stemmed from her intense desire for her family's privacy to remain intact. Not only did Jacqueline Kennedy Onassis have to worry about the media reporting on her husband's affairs, but she also had to cope with his continuous health issues and the problems they could cause to his image if they became widely known. That knowledge could hurt Kennedy's ability to lead the country successfully. From the time he was born, John F. Kennedy suffered from various ailments. During his time in the White House, he had severe migraines and back pain, along with what was later diagnosed as Addison's disease, a rare endocrine disorder which often hindered his ability to perform his duties. Unfortunately, Kennedy Onassis had to learn to deal with cameras documenting her every move, although she made no secret of hating the attention and often shooed cameras and reporters away from her family.

On top of all the other issues that surrounded their relationship, the Kennedys' attempts to have children were not immediately fruitful, leading to much heartache and worry. The stress weighed heavily upon Jacqueline, left alone to deal with her thoughts since her husband was often away on political business. Jacqueline Kennedy Onassis had a miscarriage in 1955 and gave birth to a stillborn daughter in August 1956. At long last, Kennedy Onassis gave birth to a healthy baby girl, Caroline, on 27 November 1957 after a grueling Caesarean section. With their new daughter, the couple posed proudly for the cover of the 21 April 1958 issue of *Life*, and their lives briefly appeared as perfect as the picture.

After each of the failed pregnancies, Jacqueline Kennedy Onassis slumped into a depression. Her childbearing miseries were not over, though. Kennedy Onassis became pregnant again in 1963, which led her to step away from her duties as First Lady. Five weeks ahead of her due date, on 7 August 1963, she went into labor. Patrick Bouvier Kennedy was born by emergency Caesarean section that day at Otis Air Force Base. Born prematurely, his lungs were not fully developed, so he was transferred from Cape Cod to Boston Children's Hospital for emergency treatment. After only two days, he died from hyaline membrane disease. Soon after her son's death, Jacqueline Kennedy Onassis entered another deep depression. The overwhelming grief of the past few years combined with the tragedy of losing another child had tipped her over the edge. Interestingly enough, the grief brought the Kennedy couple closer, and John F. Kennedy attempted to soothe his wife's feelings.

Jacqueline Kennedy Onassis role in her husband's life wasn't limited to providing heirs. She often accompanied him on state visits and was a fan-favorite of many foreign leaders and dignitaries. Her easy smile and cunning wit charmed officials and reporters alike. After their trip to France, *Time Magazine* noted jokingly, "There was also that fellow who came with her." Laughingly, President Kennedy said, "I am the man who accompanied Jacqueline Kennedy to Paris—and I have enjoyed it!" By herself or with her husband, she made more official visits to other countries than any of the preceding First Ladies. When the Kennedys visited Vienna, Austria, Soviet Premier Nikita Khrushchev said, "I'd like to shake her hand first," obviously referring to Jacqueline Kennedy Onassis when he was asked to pose for a picture with President John F. Kennedy. The President of Pakistan, Ayub Khan, presented her with a horse named Sardar during her tour of India and Pakistan. Kennedy Onassis let nothing gracefully represented White House, and President Kennedy appreciated his wife's stunning ability to entice other leaders.

Together, the couple stood for and promoted good policies and practices in the White House that remained as their legacy. President John F. Kennedy pushed for better working environments for American citizens, caring for their well-being and future prospects. Jacqueline Kennedy Onassis fought to preserve the history of the country she loved, starting with the White House's artifacts and interior needs. The two were powerful and determined. It was said that their hearts were larger than their pockets, as some policies created a rather large deficit for the American government. Jacqueline Kennedy Onassis made it a personal mission to preserve the history and restore the glory of the White House, and hosted fundraisers and galas to raise funding for her projects. In one fundraiser, she made White House directories and sold them as relics of her home. Over time, she gathered valuable cultural artifacts for a White House collection now considered invaluable. Today, Kennedy Onassis' efforts in the White House are revered as some of the most important historical efforts in American history. Meanwhile, President Kennedy's efforts to support a living wage and safe work conditions for Americans meant the history she worked to preserve would be meaningful.

The Kennedy family accomplished much during the short time they occupied the White House, but the presidential assassination, overshadowed the successes of John F. Kennedy's presidency. The world changed in Dallas, Texas, on 21 November 1963. The handsome young couple waved at the crowd from a convertible car as they drove past on their way to a meeting. Fireworks popped in the background. The crowd cheered on the popular, charismatic couple. Suddenly, two gunshots rang out, one striking John F. Kennedy in the chest and another in the head. Jacqueline Kennedy Onassis' reaction was evidence of her devastation.

Almost as soon as the bullet punctured John F. Kennedy's skull, Kennedy Onassis was crawling out of the car, appearing to pick up the pieces of her husband and put them together again. She remembered nothing about that moment but recalled only a sense of fear and loss. In one of the most iconic images in history, Jacqueline Kennedy Onassis was photographed in her bloodstained clothing, which she refused to remove. Her pink Chanel suit and matching pillbox hat became an image of how strength could overcome tragedy in America. Jacqueline Kennedy Onassis was a profile in courage in that moment and in the following years. After her husband's death, Jacqueline Kennedy Onassis asked her security to avoid driving past the White House. Her service detail acquiesced, allowing the First Lady to mourn without reminders of why her husband was not by her side. Although their marriage was not the fairy tale that many imagined, President John F. Kennedy and his wife, the First Lady Jacqueline Kennedy Onassis, loved one another. Kennedy Onassis was devastated by her husband's murder.

Jacqueline Kennedy Onassis recovered and built a new life with her children. She married Aristotle Onassis, an acquaintance who pursued her relentlessly, but the marriage was ultimately unsuccessful. She campaigned for Robert F. Kennedy's presidential bid, even though she had reservations about his safety. She continued to evolve, but remained steadfastly private and determined to avoid media attention. She doted on her children lovingly and invested herself in making an impact on the country that she loved. She appeared to wait for the world to be a better place.

President John F. Kennedy and First Lady Jacqueline Kennedy Onassis, icons of the administration dubbed "Camelot" remain two of the most prominent and well-remembered figures in American history. Regardless of the scandals brought to light in later years, people still remember them as harbingers of good for American society. In all, they were products of their environments—Jacqueline Kennedy Onassis as a young socialite who made the best choices available for a woman of her station and John F. Kennedy who upheld his family's long-standing tradition of impacting political change.

Part 1: John F. Kennedy

A Captivating Guide to the Life of JFK

Introduction

Gallup's List of Widely Admired People of the Twentieth Century places President John F. Kennedy in the third slot, behind Martin Luther King, Jr., and Mother Teresa. Needless to say, President Kennedy's name is one that will not soon be forgotten.[i] Many people will simply recall him as the handsome president who reigned for a short while before his unfortunate death at the hands of an assassin in Dallas, Texas. They may recall he was the youngest president to have been sworn into the presidential office or he dealt with issues such as the Cuban Missile Crisis. The general American public and the world know much about the surface of JFK's life—they know of his affairs and his ill health—but they often do not recall anything about who he was as a person or how he interacted with his wife and family.

John F. Kennedy was groomed from a young age for great things. When his older brother died, Kennedy's father began prepping JFK for life in politics. John F. Kennedy did not just happen to stumble upon fame and high positions in the American government. Rather, he struggled throughout his adult life through numerous health problems and personal issues to become the leader that people remember, and his father helped him throughout the whole process both emotionally and financially.

On 20 January 1961, John F. Kennedy was sworn into office as the thirty-fifth President of the United States of America. With that position came a heavy task: he was to lead a nation filled with people who lived on the brink of the media's explosion. President Kennedy was about to enter a world in which every detail of his life was on display. Regardless, John F. Kennedy entered his presidency with vigor. In his inaugural address, JFK said all Americans needed to serve as active citizens for their country: "Ask not what your country can do for you; ask what you can do for your country." He asked that nations across the world join together so that they may fight what he referred to as the "common enemies of man: tyranny, poverty, disease, and war itself." President Kennedy said, "All this will not be finished in the first one hundred days. Nor will it be finished in the first one thousand days, nor in the life of this Administration, nor even perhaps in our lifetime on this planet. But let us begin." Closing his speech, John F. Kennedy called for greater unity among nations of the world: "Finally, whether you are citizens of America or citizens of the world, ask of us here the same high standards of strength and sacrifice we ask of you."

Through this speech, John F. Kennedy set a new precedent for the American government. He called for change, enthusiasm, nationalism, and structure. His administration was to chart a new course in foreign affairs and domestic policy. Additionally, he spotlighted himself with this speech. While the media would have still paid great attention to his comings and goings, they now paid special mind to his daily political realities both abroad and in the United States. In contrast to Eisenhower, President Kennedy's organization was structured like that of a wheel: each spoke led directly to him as he sat in the center and controlled everything. President John F. Kennedy made quick decisions and kept a variety of experienced and inexperienced people within his Cabinet, allowing the combined knowledge to lead him in various ways and in paths that previous presidents would not have considered. "We can learn our jobs together," he said.[ii]

President John F. Kennedy preferred to live in the moment. He focused on the immediate issues affecting the country and the White House, and he found he often admonished impatient people who wanted him to ponder the deeper issues pervading the administration. When Walt Whitman Rostow, the Deputy National Security Advisor, spoke of the problem with communism's continuous growth, the young President Kennedy cut him off and asked, "What do you want me to do about that today?"[iii] Overall, President Kennedy was a short-lived but effective president. While in the presidency, he made a lot of changes in the United States. He set his goals, and he geared toward them as strongly as he could. This book will provide an outline of John F. Kennedy's life while also offering a glimpse into his thoughts on politics, the way he interacted with those he loved, and the lasting impact he made on the United States of America.

Chapter One: Childhood and Education

John Fitzgerald Kennedy entered the world on 29 May 1917 at 83 Beals Street in Brookline, Massachusetts. His father was Joseph Patrick "Joe" Kennedy, a businessman and politician. John Kennedy's mother was Rose Elizabeth Fitzgerald Kennedy. Both parents came from good, well-established backgrounds. Each of John F. Kennedy's grandfathers—P.J. Kennedy and Boston Mayor John F. Fitzgerald—were politicians in Massachusetts. Additionally, all four of his grandparents were children of Irish immigrants, so his parents had a lot in common when they married, as they had comparable backgrounds.[iv]

Young John F. Kennedy had an older brother named Joseph, Jr., and seven younger siblings: Rosemary, Kathleen, Eunice, Patricia, Robert, Jean, and Ted. For the first ten years of his life, John F. Kennedy lived in Brookline. He attended the Edward Devotion School, the Noble and Greenough Lower School, and the Dexter School through the end of his fourth-grade education. For a while, Kennedy's father was relatively absent from his children's lives. Joe Kennedy was a businessman, and his ventures kept him away from his family for long periods of time in which he resided mostly in Hollywood and on Wall Street. In September 1927, the family moved from Boston, Massachusetts, to Riverdale, Bronx, New York.[v] The family settled there, slowly integrating into New York society. From the fifth to seventh grade, John Kennedy attended the lower campus of Riverdale Country School, a private school for boys. Then, the family moved to a more suburban area in Bronxville, New York, where they found better opportunities. Here, Kennedy was a member of Boy Scouts Troop Two and attended St. Joseph's Church.[vi] Though they spent most of their time in New York, the Kennedy family maintained their home in Hyannis Port, Massachusetts, where they spent their summers and early autumn. Additionally, they had a winter home in Palm Beach, Florida, where they spent their Christmas and Easter holidays.

For eighth grade, John began attending the Canterbury School in New Milford, Connecticut, in September 1930. Unfortunately, sickness struck him, and he had to withdraw from the school in April 1931 to have an appendectomy.[vii] In the following September, he enrolled at Choate, a boarding school in Wallingford, Connecticut, for his ninth through twelfth-grade years. Living the life of a younger brother, Kennedy was overshadowed by his older brother, Joe, Jr., who had already attended Choate for two years and was both a leading student and a football player at the school. As many younger siblings do, this shadow caused him to act out with rebellious behavior to garner attention, which attracted other notoriously mischievous students. In their most memorable act, they exploded a toilet seat with a firecracker, prompting George St. John, the headmaster of the school, to assemble students in the chapel for a meeting. Once they were all seated before him, he held up the toilet seat and admonished the "muckers" who dared to "spit in our sea." From there on out, John F. Kennedy referred to his group of comrades as "The Muckers Club," which included his friend and roommate Kirk LeMoyne "Lem" Billings.[viii]

While at Choate, John fell ill once again. He was hospitalized at New Haven Hospital in 1934, and he was so sick that doctors thought that he might have had leukemia. In June 1934, he was admitted to the Mayo Clinic in Rochester, Minnesota, where he was diagnosed with colitis.[ix] In June of the following year, Kennedy graduated from Choate as 64th in his class of 112 students, which was not very impressive to anyone, but he did manage to gather a few other accolades. When he graduated, he was the business manager of the yearbook and voted "most likely to succeed."[x]

After his high school graduation, Kennedy departed on his first abroad trip in which he traveled to London with his sister, Kathleen, and his parents. His goal was to make a few connections at the London School of Economics (LSE) where he wanted to study under Harold Laski, following in his older brother's footsteps. He spent a little while in this space before succumbing to an illness that forced his return to the United States in October of the same year.

Attempting to engage with education again, Kennedy enrolled at Princeton University, where he stayed for six weeks until he was hospitalized at Peter Bent Brigham Hospital in Boston, Massachusetts, for a gastrointestinal illness. The sick young John F. Kennedy spent time convalesced in Palm Beach, Florida, at the Kennedy family's winter home. Later on, he spent the spring of 1936 on the Jay Six cattle ranch near Benson, Arizona.[xi] Here, he worked on the 40,000-acre ranch as a ranch hand, gaining some experience alongside his brother.

In September of 1936, he enrolled at Harvard, seeking education once again. His application essay read,

"The reasons that I have for wishing to go to Harvard are several. I feel that Harvard can give me a better background and a better liberal education than any other university. I have always wanted to go there, as I have felt that it is not just another college, but is a university with something definite to offer. Then too, I would like to go to the same college as my father. To be a 'Harvard man' is an enviable distinction, and one that I sincerely hope I shall attain."[xii]

Kennedy produced Harvard's "Freshman Smoker," an on-campus paper, in that year, which a reviewer called "an elaborate entertainment, which included in its cast outstanding personalities of the radio, screen, and sports world." John F. Kennedy also tried out for the football, golf, and swimming teams, earning a spot on the varsity swimming team. In addition to swimming, Kennedy sailed for the Star class, winning the 1936 Nantucket Sound Star

Championship.[xiii] He sailed to France in July of 1937 and took his convertible with him with the goal of driving around Europe.[xiv]

Later, he sailed overseas with his father and older brother in June of 1938 to work at the American Embassy in London. At this time, his father was President Franklin D. Roosevelt's United States Ambassador to the Court of St. James.[xv] In preparation for his Harvard senior honors thesis, John F. Kennedy traveled to Europe, the Balkans, the Middle East, the Soviet Union, Germany, and Czechoslovakia. He returned to London from his trip on 1 September 1939, the day that marked the beginning of World War II, when Germany invaded Poland. Kennedy's father sent him as a representative to assist in any way he could with the survivors of the *SS Athenia*. Then, John F. Kennedy flew back to the United States from Foynes, Ireland, and arrived in Port Washington, New York. All in all, he experienced a busy couple of years while attending college.

While he was an upperclassman at Harvard College, John F. Kennedy fed his growing interest in politics and philosophy, starting to learn all the information he would need later in life. His thesis, "Appeasement in Munich," which he completed in 1940, was about how Britain chose to participate in the Munich Agreement. The book outlined how Britain neglected its military's strength in the time leading up to World War II and put out a call for an Anglo-American alliance against the rising totalitarian powers. Under the title *Why England Slept*, the published thesis grew popular and hit the bestseller list.[xvi] While writing this book, Kennedy was further developing his ideologies within the political realm, starting to formulate opinions that he would carry throughout his life. The future President John F. Kennedy heavily supported the United States' intervention in World War II, which his father Joseph did not appreciate. Due to his father's isolationist beliefs, Joseph Kennedy was relieved of his duties as ambassador to the United Kingdom. This dismissal created a barrier between the Roosevelt and Kennedy families.[xvii]

John F. Kennedy graduated *cum laude* in 1940 with a Bachelor of Arts degree in government from Harvard College. Unsurprisingly, his degree concentrated heavily on international affairs. In the fall, he enrolled at the prestigious Stanford Graduate School of Business where he audited classes.[xviii] He did not spend too long at Stanford, though. He left the school in early 1941, and his father enlisted his help in writing a memoir of his three years as an American ambassador. After he finished this project, Kennedy traveled around South America for a while, visiting Ecuador, Peru, and Colombia.[xixxx]

Chapter Two: Personal Life

President John F. Kennedy's adult family life is wide open to discussion. The media surrounded them at almost all times, fascinated with JFK's handsome features and politics, while also mesmerized by Jacqueline Kennedy's style choices when they were in the White House. Needless to say, John F. Kennedy's personal life is well-known today, deriving from personal accounts, media sources, and the family's own writings. As one of the most established political families in the history of the United States, they had plenty of media coverage outside of their time in the White House, as well. The family produced a president, three senators, an ambassador, and a line of other representatives within the federal government and state governments. The Kennedy line stretches far and wide.

John F. Kennedy was introduced to Jacqueline Lee "Jackie" Bouvier (1929—1994) when he was a congressman by journalist Charles L. Bartlett at a dinner party. They married on 12 September 1953, a year after he was elected senator. In 1957, they had Caroline Bouvier Kennedy, their first child. Teasingly nicknamed "John-John" by the press, John Fitzgerald Kennedy, Jr., was born 17 days after JFK was elected president in 1960.

JFK and his wife were very popular within media culture for a myriad reasons. They were younger than any of the previous presidential families and therefore garnered much attention with their youth, youthful styles, and activities. Their faces appeared on various magazines and newspapers every day. Never at one point could any member of their family go out without finding themselves bombarded with cameras or reporters. Additionally, Kennedy was the first president to fully utilize the benefits of television. Although Eisenhower televised press conferences, John F. Kennedy was the first to have his press conferences broadcast to a live audience, which allowed for no editing of the film. In this way, the audience felt more closely connected to the president. In fact, in honor of President Kennedy's open relationship with the media, the Radio-Television News Directors Association presented him with the Paul White Award. Additionally, Jacqueline Kennedy gained notoriety and media attention for her restoration of the White House as she was continuously directing the placement of new art and furniture within the historic building. The media absolutely loved the Kennedy family.

The new family was so popular with the media their names and activities popped up numerous times in popular culture, as well. For example, The Twistin' Kings called their song "Twisting at Christmas" also by the name "Twisting at the White House," and people loved it. Additionally, Vaughn Meader's *First Family* comedy album parodied the presidential family and the administration. A popular album, it sold about four million copies. The Kennedy family also caught the attention of Marilyn Monroe, the popular actress and singer, and the woman with whom John F. Kennedy is rumored to have had an affair. At a party in Madison Square Garden on 19 May 1962, she sang "Happy Birthday, Mr. President" in celebration of JFK's upcoming 45th birthday.

While he was trying to live his life as fully as he could, John F. Kennedy was suffering from numerous health problems. Historian Robert Dallek in 2002 wrote an extensive and very detailed history of President Kennedy's health. He carefully studied a collection of papers that outlined the Kennedy family from 1955—1963. These papers included medical records such as x-rays and prescriptions, all of which were tucked away in the files of Dr. Janet Travell, the White House physician. These records indicate that John F. Kennedy suffered from a number of ailments during his time in the White

House. He had high fevers, stomach troubles, colon and prostate issues, abscesses, adrenal problems, and high cholesterol. In Dr. Travell's notes was a "Medicine Administration Record" that catalogued President Kennedy's medications in detail: "injected and ingested corticosteroids for his adrenal insufficiency; procaine shots and ultrasound treatments and hot packs for his back; Lomotil, Metamucil, paregoric, phenobarbital, testosterone, and trasentine to control his diarrhea, abdominal discomfort, and weight loss; penicillin and other antibiotics for his urinary-tract infections and an abscess; and Tuinal to help him sleep."[xxi] Needless to say, President Kennedy had a rough time while living in the nation's most famous residence as he was continuously ill.

Quite a while after John F. Kennedy's death, it was revealed he had been diagnosed with Addison's disease, a rare endocrine disorder, at age thirty while he was serving his first term in Congress. The diagnosis was made by Sir Daniel Davis at the London Clinic.[xxii] As he was elected the youngest man to ever serve as President of the United States at 43 years old, Kennedy looked as if he should have been a picture of health. Instead, he had a more complicated medical history than anyone else who had served in the same position, but it was easy to keep the secret of his ill health under wraps.

Since the media was unable to attain the same information as they can today, Kennedy was able to conceal the worst of his medical problems from the American people. The public did not know about his issues until 1976 when authors Joan and Clay Blair disclosed the information in their book *The Search for JFK*. Kennedy had come into the White House, a sick man. His family was aware of the illnesses that had plagued him as a child, and in 1947 President Kennedy collapsed while visiting England. Davis told Pamela Churchill, Kennedy's friend, "That young American friend of yours, he hasn't got a year to live."[xxiii] Upon return to the United States, President Kennedy spread the rumor that he had had a severe recurrence of malaria he contracted in the Pacific during World War II. He was safe from the judging glare of his constituents for a short while.

It is believed that during Kennedy's 1960 presidential campaign, his endocrinologist prescribed treatments with testosterone, likely as a form of long-term steroid replacement therapy and possibly because of autoimmune disease. Additionally, Kennedy experienced very severe back pain, as evidenced by a write-up about his surgery in the American Medical Association's *Archives of Surgery*. Despite his illnesses, Kennedy presented an image of health and vitality to the United States public, making them think he was well and good when, in fact, his physical body was falling apart.

During the Vienna Summit in 1961 in which he associated heavily with Soviet Premier Nikita Khrushchev, President Kennedy appeared to have been taking a multitude of drugs—animal organ cells, steroids, vitamins, hormones, amphetamines, and enzymes—which began to influence his diplomacy. Side effects of these drugs include hypertension, nervousness, mood swings, hyperactivity, and impaired judgment.[xxiv] Scholars speculate these drugs were one of the reasons he performed so poorly in front of Premier Khrushchev.

Not only did Kennedy have to deal with the stresses of his political life, but he also had to cope with his doctors' disagreements. At one time, he was seeing three or more doctors, one of whom was Max Jacobson. Known as "Dr. Feelgood" and "Miracle Max," Jacobson was a controversial figure within the medical community. He had a reputation for administering amphetamines and other strong medications to high-profile clients for quick fixes that did not usually provide long-term solutions.[xxv] Often, Kennedy's doctors disagreed as to which types of medicine would prove most beneficial for his conditions. All wanted varying amounts of exercise and health dosages. As Kennedy was a busy man and preferred immediate gratification and relief, he often followed Max Jacobson's recommendations.

In the late months of 1961, President Kennedy's physician, George Burkley, set up gym equipment in the basement of the White House, and Kennedy started a regimented schedule of exercise in which he worked his back muscles three times per week as an attempt to gain muscle strength.[xxvi] Burkley thought the other doctors' diagnoses and treatments were little more than rubbish—medically inappropriate, in other words—and removed the President of the United States from their care, thereby stopping Jacobson's use of steroids and amphetamines. After his release from these medications, Kennedy is thought to have performed more effectively in his role as leader of the United States. Dr. Ghaemi, who later studied President Kennedy's medical records, said that when Kennedy stopped taking the drugs, there was a "correlation; it is not causation, but it may not be a coincidence either" that Kennedy's leadership abilities improved.

In addition to the health problems he was experiencing and all the doctors' problems that came along with the health issues, Kennedy watched many of his family members die, which placed additional stress on him and exacerbated his poor health. In 1944, Kennedy's older brother, Joe, Jr., died at the age of 29. He was killed during an attack in Operation Aphrodite over the English Channel during World War II. The president's younger sister Rose Marie "Rosemary" Kennedy, born in 1918, suffered from intellectual disabilities and underwent a prefrontal lobotomy when she was only 23 years old. The surgery left her permanently incapacitated. Another of his younger sisters, Kathleen "Kick" Kennedy Cavendish, died in a 1948 plane crash in France. Kennedy and Jacqueline also had two deceased children and a miscarriage. Jacqueline suffered a miscarriage in 1955, which was quickly followed by a stillbirth, a daughter they named Arabella, in 1956. Then, their son, Patrick Bouvier Kennedy, died only two days after birth in August 1963.

Chapter Three: Relationship with Jackie Kennedy

Of course, it is no secret that John F. Kennedy and Jacqueline Kennedy had marital issues, as evidenced by the fact that both husband and wife were rumored to have engaged in extramarital affairs. With the president, the list of affairs begins before he was married to Jacqueline. In the 1940s, Kennedy was still a single man. During this time, he is reported to have engaged in affairs with two high-profile women, Danish journalist Inga Arvad and actress Gene Tierney.[xxvii][xxviii] These affairs gained some media speculation but were nothing in comparison to the accusations he received after his marriage to Jacqueline.

Later in his life, Kennedy was reported to have had extramarital affairs with women who ranged from celebrities to White House employees. Some include Marilyn Monroe, Gunilla von Post, Judith Campbell, Mary Pinchot Meyer, Marlene Dietrich, Mimi Alford, and even Jacqueline's secretary, Pamela Turnure. The relationship with Monroe is a bit vague, but reports claim they spent a weekend together at Bing Crosby's house in March 1962. Additionally, the White House switchboard documents calls from her during 1962.[xxix] On the other hand, his relationship with Pamela Turnure, probably the most easily accessible affair, is relatively solid information.

Somehow, most of Kennedy's affairs remained relatively unimportant to the media as the media was much less invasive during this era. Perhaps it was because his time in the White House was so short. Perhaps it was because many other important things were happening around him. Regardless, most of his affairs were not completely unearthed in detail until after his death. According to Richard Reeves, President Kennedy inspired an intense loyalty from his supporters and the members of his team, loyalty which included their discretion with "the logistics of Kennedy liaisons…[which] required secrecy and devotion rare in the annals of the energetic service demanded by successful politicians."[xxx] In other words, they kept their knowledge to themselves when questioned by the media.

Jacqueline had an important role in Kennedy's presidency. Wherever he went, she also went. She made great impressions on many foreign dignitaries and leaders, tightening United States relations with other nations. When they visited Paris on their way to the Vienna Summit, Jacqueline charmed Charles de Gaulle. After leaving, President Kennedy said he would be remembered in France as "the man who accompanied Jackie Kennedy to Paris."[xxxi]

Chapter Four: Naval Service

Due to his chronic lower back problems, John F. Kennedy was rejected from the Army's Officer Candidate School in 1940, but he was determined to make his mark on the United States military. Over the next few months, Kennedy exercised and trained to straighten his back, working to relieve the pain and problematic weakness. His hard work paid off in the end; on 24 September 1941, Kennedy joined the United States Naval Reserve with the help of the Director of the Office of Naval Intelligence (ONI), the former naval attaché to his father, Joseph Kennedy. On 26 October 1941, Kennedy was commissioned as an ensign, and he joined the staff of the Office of Naval Intelligence in Washington, D.C.

Future President John F. Kennedy moved to the Office of Naval Intelligence field office at Headquarters, Sixth Naval District, in Charleston, South Carolina, in January 1942. Continuing on the path he chose for himself, he attended the prestigious Naval Reserve Officer Training School at Northwestern University in Chicago, Illinois, from 27 July to 27 September. Then, he voluntarily entered the Motor Torpedo Boat Squadrons Training Center in Melville, Rhode Island. Kennedy was beginning to carve out a name for himself, and on 10 October, he was promoted to lieutenant junior grade, a good upgrade for the amount of time he had put into the Navy. On 2 December, he completed his training and was assigned to Motor Torpedo Squadron FOUR.

Kennedy's first command was *PT-101* and lasted from 7 December 1942 until 23 February 1943. Interestingly enough, the PT (patrol torpedo) boat had been used for training while Kennedy was an instructor at Melville. After the end of this command, he led three

Huckins PT boats—*PT-98, PT-99,* and *PT-101*—that were being relocated from MTBRON 4 in Melville, Rhode Island, back to Jacksonville Florida, alongside and in addition to the MTBRON 14. When Kennedy discovered a propeller was stuck, he dove into the cold water to fix it, but immediately fell ill. After his heroic moment, he was briefly hospitalized. When this trip reached a conclusion, Kennedy was sent to Panama and later to the Pacific theater where he commanded two more PT boats.

One of the most famous stories from this part of Kennedy's life involves his time on an island within the Solomon Islands. Kennedy was assigned to Motor Torpedo Squadron TWO in April 1943 and on 24 April took command of *PT-109*, a patrol torpedo that was based on Tulagi Island in the Solomon Islands. On the night of 1 August, while Kennedy was patrolling near New Georgia, he saw a nearby Japanese Destroyer and attempted to attack. Suddenly, *PT-109* was rammed by the destroyer Amagiri, which cut the boat in half, killing two crew members. Kennedy gathered the surviving crew members, which numbered at ten men, around the wreckage and asked them all to vote on whether they would surrender or fight. He said, "There's nothing in the book about a situation like this. A lot of you men have families, and some of you have children. What do you want to do? I have nothing to lose." They swam to a nearby island about three miles away.[xxxii] Unsurprisingly, the wreck injured Kennedy's already frail back, but he managed to swim the whole way while towing a badly burned crewman. Even more, he had to drag the crewman with a life jacket clenched in his teeth. The men later swam to a second island where they were rescued on 8 August. Kennedy and his executive officer on *PT-109*, Ensign Leonard Thom, were awarded the Purple Heart Medal for injuries and the Navy and Marine Corps Medal for heroism.

Although the medals Kennedy received were very honorable, he felt that the Navy and Marine Corps Medal was not meant for combat and asked that he should be considered for the Silver Star Medal. In 1950, the Department of the Navy offered Kennedy a Bronze Medal Star but said he would have to return his Navy and Marine Corps Medal to receive it. Kennedy declined. The Navy later offered the Bronze Star again, and Kennedy repeated his original request for consideration for the Silver Star Medal. The Navy declined. They were at a very odd standstill.

Kennedy took a while to recover from his injury, but nothing could keep him from his duties for long. Kennedy later returned to active duty, taking command of the *PT-59*—a patrol torpedo boat that was converted to a gunboat—on 1 September 1943. Kennedy was promoted to lieutenant in October, and on 2 November 1943, Kennedy's *PT-59* helped another boat to rescue eighty-seven stranded marines who were being held by the Japanese on two rescue landing crafts on the Warrior River at Choiseul Island, making Kennedy the heroic character once again.[xxxiii]

Under orders from his doctor, Kennedy was released from command of *PT-59* on 18 November, and he returned to the United States of America in early January 1944. He received treatment for his back injury, spending May to December in Chelsea Naval Hospital, and was completely released from active duty in late 1944. His condition had worsened so exponentially that he spent three more months in recovery in early 1945 at Castle Hot Springs, a resort that also functioned as a temporary military hospital in Arizona.[xxxiv]

When asked later how he became a war hero, Kennedy replied, "It was easy. They cut my PT boat in half."[xxxv] Kennedy also received the American Campaign Medal, the Asiatic-Pacific Campaign Medal with 3/16" bronze stars, and the World War II Victory Medal.

Chapter Five: Congressional Career

After his service in the United States Navy, John F. Kennedy and his father began to think about his future in the American political realm. Up until his death, Kennedy's oldest brother had been on the path for the family's political future. According to Robert Dallek, when his brother's plane crashed, Kennedy was suddenly thrust to the forefront as the oldest son and therefore the one who would have to carry on the Kennedy family's name. Therefore, the Kennedy patriarch, Kennedy's father, determined that John F. Kennedy would seek the presidency.[xxxvi]

Under the thumb and urging of Kennedy's father in 1946, the United States Representative James Michael Curley became mayor of Boston and vacated his seat in the Eleventh Congressional district in Massachusetts. John F. Kennedy easily filled the vacant seat. With the Kennedy family's finances and his father's ability to run a campaign, John F. Kennedy won the Democratic primary with 12% of the vote in competition with ten other candidates. Even though Republicans took control of the House in the 1946 elections, Kennedy beat his Republican opponent and took 76% of the vote. Alongside Richard Nixon and Joseph McCarthy, Kennedy and several other World War II veterans were elected to Congress for the first time that year.[xxxvii]

While the future President Kennedy served within the House of Representatives for six years, he was a part of the Education and Labor Committee and the Veterans' Affairs Committee. For much of his time in the House, he focused on international affairs and supported the Truman Doctrine as the best possible response to the emerging crisis of the Cold War. He supported the Immigration and Nationality

Act of 1952, which required all incoming Communists to register with the government, and he despised the "Loss of China," a phrase which referred to the Communist Party's taking over of mainland China in 1949. Additionally, he supported public housing and was strictly opposed to the Labor Management Relations Act of 1947, a movement that restricted the power of labor unions.

As early as 1949, Kennedy began preparing for his campaign for the Senate election of 1952 in which he would face the Republican three-term incumbent Henry Cabot Lodge, Jr. Again, Joseph Kennedy financed the candidacy, and during this campaign, Robert Kennedy, John F. Kennedy's younger brother, was an important member of Kennedy's team. Kennedy defeated Lodge by 70,000 votes for the Senate seat in an impressive win.

Over the next couple of years, John F. Kennedy's endurance was tested as he underwent several spinal surgeries, which left him incapacitated and unable to serve in his roles within the government. At times, he received Catholic last rites on the occasions when he was critically ill and near death. Due to his dramatic fluctuations in health, he was often absent from the Senate to the irritation and worry of other members and his constituents. In his free time of convalescence, Kennedy published *Profiles in Courage*, a book that provided life details for United States Senators who risked their careers in pursuit of their personal beliefs. For this book, he won the Pulitzer Prize for Biography in 1957. Some rumors said his speechwriter and adviser Ted Sorensen helped to write the book, which was confirmed in Sorensen's 2008 autobiography.

During the 1956 Democratic National Convention, the future President Kennedy delivered the nominating speech for the party's presidential nominee, Adlai Stevenson II.[xxxviii] Stevenson preferred the convention select the vice-presidential nominee, and Kennedy finished second in the balloting with Senator Estes Kefauver of Tennessee coming ahead of him. Regardless, Kennedy still gained national exposure as a result of his run for the nomination.

Kennedy had other things to worry about without the stress of the vice-presidential nomination. During his time in the Senate, President Eisenhower presented the bill for the Civil Rights Act of 1957.[xxxix] Many people thought Kennedy was attempting to appease Southern Democratic opponents of the bill when he cast a procedural vote. In the end, he voted for Title III of the act, which would have granted the Attorney General powers to enjoin, but the Majority Leader, future vice president, and president Lyndon B. Johnson, agreed to let the provision die as a compromise measure. Kennedy then voted for Title IV, which was dubbed the "Jury Trial Amendment." Quite a few Civil Rights advocates said that vote would weaken the act, rather than give it more power. Eventually, Kennedy supported a final compromise bill, which passed in September 1957.[xl]

Kennedy was re-elected to a second term in the Senate in 1958, successfully defeating his Republican opponent, Boston lawyer Vincent J. Celeste, by a huge margin of 874, 608 votes in all. At that time, this election held the largest ever margin in Massachusetts politics. During the re-election campaign, Kennedy's press secretary, Robert E. Thompson, helped Kennedy's fame soar; Thompson put together a film entitled *The U.S. Senator John F. Kennedy Story*, which showcased Kennedy's life in the White House, the inner workings of his job, and his home life with his family. At the time, the film was considered a comprehensive overview of Kennedy's story. After his re-election to the Senate, Kennedy began preparing for a 1960 presidential campaign, already looking forward to ways in which he could change America for the better.[xli]

Chapter Six: 1960 Presidential Race

On 2 January 1960, John F. Kennedy announced his intentions to run for the Democratic presidential nomination. Some people questioned his youth and inexperience, but Kennedy won over large crowds of supporters with his eloquence and charisma. JFK's biggest obstacle in winning the nomination was not his inexperience or his youth but rather his Catholicism because the religion represented a minority in America. Many Americans held anti-Catholic attitudes and looked down on his religious choices, but Kennedy's vocal and heavy support of the separation of church and state helped to calm the problem. Kennedy's religion helped him win a devoted following from many Catholic voters.

A few other obstacles were represented by Kennedy's challengers for the Democratic nomination: Adlai Stevenson, Senator Hubert Humphrey, and Senate Majority Leader Lyndon B. Johnson. Kennedy worked rather hard. He purposefully traveled all over the country to build his support among the nation's democratic supporters and voters. Party officials controlled most of the delegates, but Kennedy spent a good amount of time campaigning in states that also held primaries, seeking to win several, which would boost his chances of winning the Democratic nomination. Effectively snuffing Humphrey's chances of winning the presidency, Kennedy won the Wisconsin and West Virginia primaries, surprising and impressing many Democrats. Still, at the beginning of the 1960 Democratic National Convention, people were not sure as to who would win the nomination when it boiled down to counting the votes.[xlii]

Upon entering the convention, Kennedy was the nominee with the most delegates, but the gap in numbers was not enough to ensure a clear win in the nomination. Stevenson, who was nominated to run for the Democratic Party in both 1952 and 1956, was popular in the party, and Johnson was not far behind him. Kennedy also faced a roadblock with former president Harry S. Truman, who worried that Kennedy was too inexperienced for the job of President of the United States. Trying to avoid a second ballot, Kennedy made sure his campaign was well-organized and strong, resulting in Kennedy's name coming out on top for the presidential nomination on the first ballot without having to go to a second.[xliii] Although his supporters and his brother were opposed to the idea, Kennedy chose Lyndon B. Johnson as his vice-presidential nominee, assuring himself the Texan Senator could help him win support from the states in the South.[xliv]

When he accepted the presidential nomination, Kennedy delivered his famous "New Frontier Speech": "For the problems are not all solved, and the battles are not all won—and we stand today on the edge of a New Frontier…But the New Frontier of which I speak is not a set of promises—it is a set of challenges. It sums up not what I intend to offer the American people but what I intend to ask of them." On lists of great speeches, Kennedy's words in this particular speech often pop up as some of the most moving and inspirational in American history.

On the Republican side of the voters' list was Republican nominee Richard Nixon, who already held experience in the White House as the incumbent vice president. During their talks with voters, the two elected nominees focused on some of the following major issues: the dragging economy, Kennedy's Roman Catholicism, the Soviet space and missile programs, and the Cuban Revolution. Addressing his Catholic background, Kennedy told the Greater Houston Ministerial Association on 12 September 1960, "I am not the Catholic candidate for president. I am the Democratic Party candidate for president who also happens to be a Catholic. I do not speak for my Church on public matters—and the Church does not speak for me." Quite a few times, Kennedy was bristled when people assumed he would run the country poorly because of his religious background. He often threw the question back at voters, asking if they thought one-fourth of American citizens were of a lower class based purely on their Catholicism. Driving the point home, he said, "No one asked me my religion [while serving in the Navy] in the South Pacific."[xlv]

Kennedy squared off against Nixon in September and October during the first televised presidential debates in the history of the United States. Unfortunately for Nixon, he did not perform well during the televised programs. He had a sore, injured leg, and his short beard was sweating. He looked uncomfortable, tense, and ill-prepared. On the other hand, Kennedy made use of the makeup services and appeared relaxed in front of the camera, leading the television audience to favor his performance. Funny enough, radio listeners assumed that Nixon won the debate or that it was a tie since they could not see his appearance. At this moment in time, television began playing a dominant role in politics, allowing Kennedy's good looks and suave personality to help him in the presidential race.

After the first debate, Kennedy's campaign gained momentum, and he took over the lead in the polls. In the popular vote, Kennedy beat Nixon by only two-tenths of one percent, but the Electoral College voted in at 303 for Kennedy and 219 for Nixon. Kennedy would have garnered even more votes if 14 electors in Mississippi and Alabama had not refused to support him on the grounds of his strong support for the Civil Rights Movement. Along with one elector for Oklahoma, electors in Mississippi and Alabama voted for Senator Harry F. Byrd of Virginia instead. Regardless, Kennedy found his space in the presidential office. He became the youngest person ever to be elected as president, even though Theodore Roosevelt was younger when he took office after William McKinley's untimely death in 1901.[xlvi]

Chapter Seven: Presidency—Foreign Policy

John F. Kennedy did not have much time to rest between his campaign and his first days in the White House. As soon as he entered the presidency, he engaged with numerous issues. Confrontations with the Soviet Union were not the least of his worries as the earliest stages of the Cold War were setting in. In 1961, Kennedy planned a summit to meet with Soviet Premier Nikita Khrushchev. Unfortunately, the president made an ill first impression when he aggressively reacted to one of Khrushchev's speeches on the Cold War. Although Khrushchev intended the speech to reach out to the Soviet Union's domestic audiences, Kennedy took it as a personal challenge, which raised tensions leading up to the Vienna Summit of June 1961.[xlvii] Charles de Gaulle, the French president, and Kennedy met in Paris on Kennedy's way to the Summit. Here, de Gaulle suggested that Kennedy ignore Krushchev's abrasiveness and instead focus on the important matters at hand. Maybe if Kennedy had taken his advice, the meeting would have gone more smoothly.

Kennedy and Khrushchev met in Vienna on 4 June 1961. The president left the meeting filled with anger and disappointment, feeling he had allowed Premier Khrushchev to bully him verbally. Khrushchev was duly impressed with Kennedy's intelligence but thought he was a weak and ineffective leader. While in the meeting, Kennedy brought up a sensitive topic: a proposed treaty between East Berlin and Moscow. He clearly stated that any treaty of the sort would be regarded as an act of war since it interfered with the United States' access rights in West Berlin. Regardless of Kennedy's threats, he soon discovered after he returned home the Soviet Union leaders were announcing their intentions to sign a treaty with East Berlin. Kennedy began preparing the country for a nuclear war; his personal belief was nuclear war had about a one-in-five chance of happening, so he wanted to make sure he was prepared for the inevitable.[xlviii]

During the weeks following the Vienna Summit, over 20,000 people who feared the Soviets' statements began to flee from East Berlin toward the western sector. Dean Acheson, Secretary of State to Harry S. Truman and unofficial advisor to John F. Kennedy, recommended a military buildup for the United States of America. Taking his advice, Kennedy announced in July 1961 his decision to increase the defense budget by 3.5 billion dollars, in addition to adding more than 200,000 additional troops. The United States claimed an attack on West Berlin would function as an attack on America, as well. John F. Kennedy's speech announcing this information received an 85% approval rating from American citizens, showing the country appreciated his firm stance.[xlix]

In the month after President Kennedy broadcasted his plans, the Soviets and East Berliners began creating a blockade, allowing no one in East Berlin to cross over into West Berlin. They built barbed wire fences around the city, which quickly escalated to become the Berlin Wall. Kennedy chose to ignore this issue as long as access between the opposing sides of Berlin was still available. Soon, though, people in West Berlin began to lose hope in the United States' defense of their wavering position. In an attempt to restore confidence, Kennedy sent Vice President Lyndon B. Johnson and a host of military personnel to convoy through West Germany in a show of strength, a journey which included passage through Soviet-armed checkpoints.[l]

On 5 May 1960, President Kennedy addressed American concerns about the Cold War at Saint Anselm College. He spoke on America's conduct in the rising War, detailing how he believed American foreign policy should be conducted toward African nations and claimed to support modern African nationalism: "For we, too, founded a new nation on revolt from colonial rule."

While Kennedy was attempting to deal with Russia, he also had another country about which to worry: Cuba. When Eisenhower was in the presidency, he and his administration created a plan to overthrow Fidel Castro's dictatorial rule in Cuba. The plan required the Central Intelligence Agency (CIA) to team with the United States military in efforts to invade Cuba with a counter-revolutionary insurgency that was made up of anti-Castro, United States-trained Cuban exiles that followed the lead of CIA paramilitary officers. Their goal was to invade Cuba, create an uprising among the Cuban people, and remove Castro from power.[li] The plan was passed along to Kennedy, who approved it on 4 April 1961. The administration began hashing out the details.

Dubbed the Bay of Pigs Invasion, the planned infiltration began on 17 April 1961. The Brigade 2506, which consisted of 1,500 United States-trained Cubans, landed on the island, with no United States air support providing backup. The director of the Central Intelligence Agency, Allen Dulles, said later the leaders on the ground assumed President Kennedy would authorize anything that would allow success for the troops once they were landed and on the ground.[lii] That did not seem to be the case, though. Within two days of their landing, the Cuban government managed to capture or kill all the invading exiles, which meant that Kennedy gained the responsibility of negotiating for the release of over 1,100 survivors, a goal for which he did not have the time or patience. Twenty months later, Cuba made an agreement with the United States government in which they released the exiles in exchange for 53 million dollars' worth of food and medicine.[liii] The incident did prove one good thing, though: Fidel Castro grew wary of the United States in fear that they would send invaders again in the future.

Biographer Richard Reeves argues that during the Bay of Pigs Invasion and its execution, Kennedy maintained a larger focus on the political repercussions of his plan, paying less attention to the military issues that came along with it. When the plan failed, he became quite aggravated and assumed people were conspiring against him to make him look bad as a leader of the United States.[liv] Regardless, President Kennedy took responsibility for the failure. He said, "We got a big kick in the leg, and we deserved it. But maybe we'll learn something from it."[lv] With few other options, the White House created a Special Group—led by Robert Kennedy and including Edward Lansdale and Secretary Robert McNamara—with the specific goal to take down Fidel Castro's reign through the use of espionage, sabotage, and other covert affairs. In reality, those tactics were never pursued.[lvi]

On 14 October 1962, Kennedy's two largest problems in foreign affairs—Cuba and Russia—came together in a conspiracy. Central Intelligence Agency U-2 spy planes were able to successfully photograph intermediate-range ballistic missile sites that the Soviets were building in Cuba. President Kennedy saw the pictures on 16 October. Along with a team of advisors, Kennedy reached the conclusion that the missiles were offensive and dangerous, therefore posing an immediate nuclear threat to the country and the world.[lvii] Unfortunately, a problem arose, blocking any further action. The United States had a dilemma: if they attacked the missile sites, their actions might prompt a nuclear war, but if they did nothing, the country would fall under the threat of nearby nuclear weapons while also appearing weak to the rest of the world in their defense of the hemisphere. Since Kennedy had already presented himself as a weak leader to Khrushchev, he had a lot to prove after the Vienna Summit and did not want to appear weak in this aspect, as well.[lviii]

Within the National Security Council (NSC), over a third of the members preferred a surprise air assault on the Soviet missile sites, but other members thought this action would be too reminiscent of what they called "Pearl Harbor in reverse."[lix] Some of the international community members who were privy to this possible plan thought it might seem a bit like the pot calling the kettle black in light of

Eisenhower's placement of PGM-19 Jupiter missiles in Italy and Turkey in 1958. Additionally, there was no way to guarantee that an assault would prove 100 percent effective.[lx] After the National Security Council voted on the issue, President Kennedy determined that the United States would impose a naval quarantine. Then, on 22 October, he sent a message to Khrushchev with the plan included before announcing the decision publicly on television.[lxi]

According to the new plan, the United States Navy, beginning on 24 October, would halt and do a thorough inspection of all Soviet ships that arrived near Cuba, attempting to keep the Cuban government from gaining any more nuclear power than they already had. The Organization of American States, which consisted of 35 independent states of the Americas, provided unanimous support for removing the Soviet missiles, so the United States was not alone in its goals. President Kennedy and Soviet Premier Khrushchev exchanged two sets of letters but produced no real results. General U. Thant, the Secretary of the United Nations, requested that both parties try to settle back for a while in a cooling-off period before making any rash decisions. Khrushchev agreed to follow Thant's advice, but Kennedy did not.[lxii]

Only one time did the United States Navy have to stop a Soviet-flagged ship to board to search; needless to say, the plan was less fruitful than the United States government expected, but it did what it needed to do. Soon after, on 28 October, Khrushchev agreed to dismantle and disband the missile sites in Cuba under the watchful eye of United Nations inspectors. Publicly, the United States promised they would refrain from ever invading Cuba and, privately, they agreed to also remove their Jupiter missiles from their locations in Italy and Turkey, so they did not encounter the same issues again in the case of another nuclear crisis.[lxiii] At the end of the crisis, Kennedy experienced a rise in his credibility and approval ratings.[lxiv]

Kennedy was also dealing with communistic issues in Latin America. President Kennedy said, "Those who make peaceful revolution impossible will make violent revolution inevitable." In light of the perceived communist threat in Latin America, he aimed toward creating the Alliance for Progress, which provided aid to those Latin American countries that sought to garner greater human rights outside of the rule of communist governments.[lxv] He and the Governor of Puerto Rico, Luis Muñoz Marín, worked closely together to develop the Alliance for Progress with the goal of the Commonwealth of Puerto Rico's gaining autonomy.

President Kennedy had inherited the Eisenhower administration's plans to assassinate Fidel Castro. In addition to this tyrant, they were also aiming to eradicate Rafael Trujillo in the Dominican Republic, which created another issue within Kennedy's politics. Kennedy made sure the CIA knew any such plans must include plausible deniability from the United States government. In the public eye, Kennedy denied the government had planned an assassination attempt of any sort.[lxvi] In June of 1961, the leader of the Dominican Republic was assassinated; following his death, the Undersecretary of State, Chester Bowles, led a cautious reaction by the nation. Robert Kennedy, thinking quickly and seeing an opportunity for the United States, called Bowles a "gutless bastard" to his face in an attempt to create a public distaste for him.[lxvii]

Kennedy asked Congress to create the Peace Corps. Robert Sargent Shriver, John F. Kennedy's brother-in-law, was the first director of the Peace Corps.[lxviii] Within this program, American citizens volunteered to assist underdeveloped nations in education, healthcare, construction, and farming. By March 1963, the organization had grown to 5,000 members, then 10,000 in 1964.[lxix] Since 1961, over 200,000 American citizens have joined the Peace Corps, which provides services in 139 countries.[lxx]

When a new president arrives at the White House, they are briefed by the previous President of the United States on current issues and threats. When President Kennedy met with Eisenhower, the former president emphasized the communist threat in Southeast Asia, saying it needed immediate attention as a priority for the White House. Eisenhower said Laos was "the cork in the bottle." Then in March 1961, Kennedy altered the policy surrounded Laos, saying the country should be neutral, rather than free, and that Vietnam, not Laos, should be the center of America's focus as the tripwire for the spread of communism in the area.[lxxi]

President Kennedy sent Vice President Lyndon B. Johnson in May 1961 to meet with the President of South Vietnam, Ngo Dinh Diem. Johnson guaranteed the United States would provide more aid in creating a fighting force to resist the communists. After this meeting, President Kennedy announced there was to be a change in policy regarding the United States' partnership with Diem; they would join to defeat the communism that was overtaking the government in South Vietnam.[lxxii] During his administration, Kennedy continued to create policies that provided political and economic support, along with military advice and support, for the South Vietnamese government.[lxxiii] In late 1961, the Viet Cong garnered more attention on the political world scene as they seized the provincial capital of Phuoc Vinh.[lxxiv] In reaction, Kennedy increased the number of United States Special Forces and military advisors, which he utilized almost exclusively in Vietnam, from 11,000 to 16,000 over the course of two years, but he did not command a full-scale deployment of troops.[lxxv] A year and a half later, after Kennedy's death, President Lyndon B. Johnson, sent the first combat troops to Vietnam, heavily escalating the involvement of the United States. After this, forces reached 184,000 in number then 536,000 in 1968.

At the beginning of 1962, President Kennedy increased involvement in Vietnam upon signing the National Security Action Memorandum, "Subversive Insurgency (War of Liberation)."[lxxvi] Within the United States, strong supporters and strong opponents voiced their opinions on the subject of engaging with Vietnam. Dean Rusk, the Secretary of State under President Kennedy, strongly supported the involvement of the United States in Vietnam. Kennedy spoke of the situation in

Vietnam in April 1963: "We don't have a prayer of staying in Vietnam. Those people hate us. They are going to throw our asses out of there at any point. But I can't give up that territory to the communists and get the American people to re-elect me."[lxxvii] Despite the weighty support of the United States, the Vietnamese military was not very effective in combatting the pro-communist Viet Cong forces. President Kennedy's crisis began with this realization. Soon after, the United States clergy on the Ministers' Vietnam Committee began expressing the first formal anti-Vietnam sentiments.[lxxviii]

In September, the White House met to discuss the impending disaster in Vietnam. General Victor Krulak of the Department of Defense and Joseph Mendenhall of the State Department provided updated assessments to the meeting after they engaged personal inspections on the ground. Krulak argued the military fight against the communists was going well, while Mendenhall said the country was slowly losing the United States' influence. After hearing their testimonies, Kennedy, unaware the two men were not speaking with one another is reported as asking, "Did you two gentlemen visit the same country?"[lxxix]

In an effort to reconcile the competing reports and to manage to formulate a policy based on fact, President Kennedy appointed Defense Secretary McNamara and General Maxwell D. Taylor to a mission in Vietnam. McNamara and Taylor were to visit the country with a goal that "emphasized the importance of getting to the bottom of the differences in reporting from U.S. representatives in Vietnam."[lxxx] Vietnam's vice president, Nguyen Ngoc Tho, told Taylor and McNamara that the military was not succeeding at all. In light of this information, Kennedy insisted that troops begin withdrawing with 1,000 leaving by the end of the year and all dispersing by 1965 since he felt like he was wasting his time and resources.

In October, international reports began suggesting that a coup against the Diem government was brewing. President Kennedy instructed the

United States offer secret assistance to the coup as long as the plan did not involve assassination and the United States could deny involvement.[lxxxi] As the coup grew closer, Kennedy ordered all cables should be routed through him. He wanted complete control of the responses from the United States but also wanted to avoid affiliation through a paper trail, which put him in a difficult space.[lxxxii] Finally, South Vietnamese generals overthrew the Diem government on 1 November 1963, resulting in the arrest and killing of Diem and Nhu. President Kennedy was surprised by the assassinations but was informed the deaths were necessary since the time frame would not have worked out in any other way.[lxxxiii]

Initially, news of the coup instilled a new sense of confidence both in America and South Vietnam, and both countries considered that the war might be won. Before leaving for his ill-timed trip to Dallas, President Kennedy told Michael Forrestal, who was his National Security Advisor, that "after the first of the year, [he wanted] an in-depth study of every possible option [for the war], including how to get out of there…to review this whole thing from the bottom to the top." Forrestal translated this message as the following: "It was devil's advocate stuff."[lxxxiv]

Many historians have various opinions as to whether Kennedy's living would have escalated the Vietnam issue. In the film *The Fog of War*, Secretary of Defense McNamara said that Kennedy was strongly opposed to pulling the United States out of Vietnam after the 1964 election, assuming he would have won.[lxxxv] Lyndon Johnson claimed on tape, though, that Kennedy was planning to withdraw troops. Robert Kennedy said in 1964 that if South Vietnam had been on the brink of defeat, he and his brother would have had to "face that when we came to it." In fact, at the time of Kennedy's death, there was no clear decision about the United States future policy on how to deal with Vietnam.[lxxxvi] Theodore Sorensen wrote in 2008, "I would like to believe that Kennedy would have found a way to withdraw all American instructors and advisors [from Vietnam]. But even someone who knew JFK as well as I did can't be certain because I do not believe he knew in his last weeks what he was going to do…[Vietnam] was the only foreign policy problem handed off by JFK to his successor in no better, and possibly worse, shape than it was when he inherited it."[lxxxvii]

What we do know is that Kennedy presented the commencement address at American University in Washington, D.C., on 10 June 1963. In this speech, the President outlined a plan to curb nuclear weapons. Additionally, he "laid out a hopeful, yet realistic route for world peace at a time when the U.S. and Soviet Union faced the potential for an escalating nuclear arms race." President Kennedy wished to

"discuss a topic on which too often ignorance abounds and the truth is too rarely perceived—yet it is the most important topic on earth: world peace…I speak of peace because of the new face of war…in an age when a singular nuclear weapon contains ten times the explosive force delivered by all the allied forces in the Second World War…an age when the deadly poisons produced by a nuclear exchange would be carried by wind and air and soil and sea to the far corners of the globe and to generations yet unborn…I speak of peace, therefore, as the necessary rational end of rational men…world peace, like community peace, does not require that each man love his neighbor—it requires only that they live together in mutual tolerance…our problems are man-made—therefore they can be solved by man. And man can be as big as he wants."[lxxxviii]

In his announcement, the president made two important notes: The Soviets wanted to negotiate a nuclear test ban treaty, and the United States postponed planned atmospheric tests.[lxxxix]

In light of France's attempt to build a Franco-West German counterweight to the American and Soviet spheres of influence, Kennedy gave a public speech in West Berlin to remind the world of America's commitment to Germany and to criticizing communism.

The response was ecstatic and positive.[xc] Utilizing the Berlin Wall as an example of communism's failures, Kennedy said, "Freedom has many difficulties, and democracy is not perfect. But we have never had to put a wall up to keep our people in, to prevent them from leaving us." The speech is known for the phrase *Ich bin ein Berliner*, which translates to "I am a citizen of Berlin." Over one million people showed up on the streets of Berlin to hear the speech, and Kennedy later remarked to Ted Sorensen, "We'll never have another day like this one, as long as we live."[xci]

Additionally, Kennedy kept a caring eye on Israel during his presidency. He initiated security ties with the country, receiving credit as the founder of the United States-Israeli military alliance. He also ended the Eisenhower and Truman administrations' and enforced an arms embargo on Israel. He said in 1960, "Israel will endure and flourish. It is the child of hope and the home of the brave. It can neither be broken by adversity nor demoralized by success. It carries the shield of democracy, and it honors the sword of freedom." Kennedy described the United States' protection of Israel as a moral and national obligation. In 1962, the President offered the first informal security guarantees to Israel and was the first president to allow Israel to buy advanced United States weaponry and to provide support for Israeli policies, such as their water project on the Jordan River, against Arab neighbors.[xcii]

President Kennedy ran into a few roadblocks with Israel during his dealings with the government. He encountered tensions with the Israeli leadership over their production of nuclear materials in Dimona; the President believed the production could instigate a nuclear arms race in the Middle East. In the beginning, the Israeli government denied the existence of a nuclear plant, and David Ben-Gurion, in a speech to the Israeli Knesset on 21 December, said that the Beersheba nuclear plant's purpose was for "research in problems of arid zones and desert flora and fauna."[xciii] Upon meeting with Kennedy in New York, Ben-Gurion claimed that Dimona would provide nuclear power for desalinization and other peaceful endeavors "for the time being."[xciv]

Later, Kennedy wrote a letter to Ben-Gurion, saying he was nervous about proceedings and that American support was on the line if Israel did not provide reliable information on their nuclear program. Ben-Gurion repeated his previous peaceful promises that all would be well, but the Israeli government resisted American insistence they open their nuclear facilities to inspection by the International Atomic Energy Agency (IAEA). By 1962, though, the United States and Israeli governments agreed to an annual inspection regime. The American leading the inspection team said the goal was to find "ways to not reach the point of taking action against Israel's nuclear weapons program."[xcv]

Unfortunately, a science attaché in the Tel Aviv embassy shared that the Israeli government temporarily shut down part of the Dimona facility to mislead the visiting American scientists.[xcvi] According to journalist and political writer Seymour Hersh, the Israeli government set up false rooms for the visiting Americans to view. Abe Feinberg, and Israeli lobbyist said, "It was part of my job to tip them off that Kennedy was insisting on [an inspection]."[xcvii] Hersh argued the conducted inspections "guaranteed that the whole procedure would be little more than a whitewash, as the President and his senior advisors had to understand: the American inspection team would have to schedule its visits well in advance and with the full acquiescence of Israel."[xcviii] Marc Trachtenberg who is a professor of international relations at UCLA, has argued that "Although well aware of what the Israelis were doing, Kennedy chose to take this as satisfactory evidence of Israeli compliance with America's non-proliferation policy."[xcix] After much back and forth, Dimona was never placed under IAEA safeguards, and attempts to force Israel to adhere to the Nuclear Non-Proliferation Treaty continued until 1968.

Following the overthrow of the Iraqi monarchy on 14 July 1958 and the declaration of a republic government under Brigadier Abd al-

Karim Qasim, relations between Iraq and the United States grew strained.[c] A couple of years after the new government was installed, Qasim installed troops on the border between Iraq and Kuwait on 25 June 1961, saying that Kuwait was "an indivisible part of Iraq," which caused a brief "Kuwait Crisis." President Kennedy, with help from the United Kingdom's endeavor to bring the dispute to the United Nations Security Council, dispatched a United States Navy task force to Bahrain. The situation was finally resolved in October, but the Qasim government passed Public Law 80 in December 1961, restricting the British- and American-owned Iraq Petroleum Company (IPC)'s concessionary holding to the oil-producing areas.

Robert Komer, the Senior National Security Council adviser, worried that if the IPC ceased production, Qasim might attempt to take Kuwait or look to Russia for help. The State Department in April 1962 issued new guidelines on Iraq with the intention to increase American influence. President Kennedy attempted to take control of the situation and instructed the CIA to make preparations for a military coup against Qasim.[ci] On 8 February 1963, the anti-imperialist and anti-communist Iraqi Ba'ath Party overthrew and then executed Qasim in a violent coup. Some rumors say that the CIA organized and executed the coup, but declassified documents and former CIA agents' testimonies claim that America was not directly involved even though the CIA was, indeed, searching the Iraqi military for a replacement for Qasim. Overall, the Kennedy administration was pleased with the outcome of the coup and approved a 55 million-dollar arms deal for Iraq.[cii]

Chapter Eight: Domestic Policy

When the new President John F. Kennedy entered the Oval Office, he entered a domestic program contract, as well. He had a lot of promises to keep: the "New Frontier" was in its earliest stages. This new domestic program promised to provide federal funding for medical care for the elderly; education, economic aid for rural areas, and, finally, government intervention to halt the recession ravaging the country. Additionally, President Kennedy was ambitious in promising to end racial discrimination through his endorsement of the Voter Education Project (VEP), which actually produced little to no progress in states such as Mississippi where racism was rampant; the "VEP concluded that discrimination was so entrenched."

When President Kennedy gave his State of the Union address in 1963, he proposed a substantial tax reform, along with a reduction in income tax rates from the 20-90% range to a lower 14-65% range. He also proposed lowering corporate tax rates from 53% to 47% and that the top rate should be set at 70% if deductions were not eliminated for high-income earners. Speaking to the Economic Club of New York in 1963, President Kennedy said, "The paradoxical truth [is] that tax rates are too high and revenues too low, and the soundest way to raise revenue in the long term is to lower rates now."[ciii] Congress did not actually move toward these goals until 1964 after Kennedy's death when they lowered the top individual rate to 70% and the top corporate rate to 48%.

Coming into power, President Kennedy ended an era of tight fiscal policies, creating monetary policies that were looser than previous presidents' ideas in order to lower interest rates and encourage economic growth.[civ] Even with his efforts, Kennedy was the first president to work with a government that topped the 100 billion-dollar mark on the national budget deficit. Additionally, in 1961, he led the country's first non-war, non-recession deficit.[cv] Regardless, the economy accelerated noticeably during his presidency after being in two recessions during three years as it turned and prospered under the Kennedy administration. According to the United States Department of Commerce, the rate of growth in GDP and industry continued until around 1969 and has yet to repeat this trend over such a sustained period of time.

During Kennedy's presidency, the United States steel industry gained attention. Robert Kennedy argued the steel executives determined together that they would fix prices, saying that "We're going for broke…their expense accounts, where they've been and what they've been doing…the FBI is to interview them all…we can't lose this."[cvi] Administration worked with U.S. Steel, convincing them to rescind the increase in prices. The *Wall Street Journal* said that the administration acted "by naked power, by threats, by agents of the state security police," and Charles Reich, a Yale law professor, said in an article in *The New Republic* that the administration violated civil liberties by so quickly calling a grand jury to indict U.S. Steel for collusion.[cvii] On the other hand, a writer for the *New York Times* praised President Kennedy's reactions, saying the steel industry's price increase "imperils the economic welfare of the country by inviting a tidal wave of inflation." The Bureau of Budget told another story: a report stated that the price increase would have allowed for a net gain in GDP, along with a net budget surplus.[cviii] Additionally, the stock market dropped 10% after the administration chose to take action against the steel industry.[cix]

President Kennedy made a few other stirs in administration policy, as well, one of which included the last federal execution prior to *Furman v. Georgia*, a 1972 case that led to a moratorium on federal executions. A federal court in Iowa sentenced Victor Feguer to death, and he was executed on 15 March 1963. Believing this mandated execution was too much, President Kennedy commuted a death sentence a military court imposed on seaman Jimmie Henderson on 12 February 1962, instead suggesting that life in prison would serve just as well. Then on 22 March 1962, Kennedy signed HR5243 (PL87-423) into law, which abolished the mandatory death penalty for first-degree murder in the District of Columbia, which was the only place in the United States that inflicted this penalty.

Kennedy, claiming he would solve the issues of state-sanctioned racial discrimination in the United States, took on a large and important burden when he entered the presidential office. As institutional racism was one of the most obvious and pressing domestic issues of the 1960s, President Kennedy had his hands full. Up until this point, Jim Crow segregation was still the established and followed law in the Deep South.[cx] In 1954, the Supreme Court of the United States ruled during the case of *Brown v. Board of Education* that racial segregation in public schools was unconstitutional. Regardless, many southern states ignored the Supreme Court's decision, along with keeping public spaces such as buses, theaters, bathrooms, beaches, restaurants, and courtrooms segregated.[cxi]

Kennedy took a strong stand, verbally supporting racial integration and Civil Rights. During his 1960 campaign, he called Coretta Scott King—the wife of the Reverend Martin Luther King, Jr., who was in jail at the time for attempting to integrate a department store lunch counter. Robert Kennedy also took action, calling Georgia Governor Ernest Vandiver to obtain MLK's release from prison; his brother's candidacy provided him additional authority in his request.[cxii] Historian Carl M. Brauer argues that attempting to pass any Civil Rights legislation in 1961 would have proved futile due to Southern Democratic control of congressional legislation.[cxiii] During his first year in office, President Kennedy attempted to integrate the White House, as well, appointing many black American citizens to office, including his May appointment of Thurgood Marshall, a Civil Rights attorney, to the federal bench.[cxiv]

President Kennedy said in January 1961, during his first State of the Union Address, "The denial of constitutional rights to some of our fellow Americans on account of race—at the ballot box and elsewhere—disturbs the national conscience, and subjects us to the change of world opinion that our democracy is not equal to the high promise of our heritage." Kennedy knew that the grassroots aspect of the Civil Rights Movement would easily anger most white people in the South, making it harder to pass Civil Rights laws, including anti-poverty legislation, in Congress; therefore, he distanced himself from it.[cxv]

Robert Kennedy suggested his brother needed to be concerned with foreign issues, rather than domestic policy and said that the administrations' early priority was to "keep the president out of this civil rights mess." Participants in the Civil Rights Movement criticized President Kennedy, saying he was lukewarm on issues, especially of concern to the Freedom Riders who were organizing an integrated public transportation system in the South and were repeatedly intimidated and harmed by white men engaging in mob violence, which included law enforcement officers at federal and state levels. In reaction, Kennedy assigned federal marshals to protect the Freedom Riders, a move which the Riders did not consider enough in light of the fact that he could have done much more.[cxvi] Speaking for the president, Robert Kennedy advised that the Freedom Riders "get off the buses and leave the matter to peaceful settlement in courts."[cxvii] The Kennedys thought that sending federal troops would exacerbate the problem and would stir up "hated memories of Reconstruction" among white conservatives in the South.[cxviii]

On 6 March 1961, Kennedy signed Executive Order 10925, which stated government contractors must "take affirmative action to ensure that applicants are employed and that employees are treated during employment without regard to their race, creed, color, or national origin," therefore establishing the President's Committee on Equal Employment Opportunity. Unhappy with the president's reluctance to address directly the issue of segregation at an admirable pace, the Reverend Martin Luther King, Jr. and his fellow fighters for justice produced a document in 1962 that called on President Kennedy to follow Abraham Lincoln's example by using an Executive Order to make Civil Rights a Second Emancipation Proclamation. President Kennedy did not follow the advice and did not execute the order.

A pivotal point in the Civil Rights Movement occurred in September 1962 when James Meredith enrolled at the University of Mississippi. When he arrived on campus, he was prohibited from entering. Attorney General Robert Kennedy's response was to send 400 federal marshals, and President Kennedy sent 3,000 troops after the campus situation grew violent in nature.[cxix] After the Ole Miss Riot of 1962 ended, two people were dead, and dozens were injured, but Meredith finally enrolled for class. President Kennedy immediately regretted his choice not to send more troops earlier and reconsidered his ideas on how to deal with integration in the South. On 20 November 1962, Kennedy finally signed Executive Order 11063, which prohibited racial discrimination in federally-supported housing or "related facilities."[cxx]

In the White House, Civil Rights conversations were getting heated. President Kennedy in early 1963 told the Reverend Martin Luther King, Jr. his thoughts on Civil Rights legislation: "If we get into a long fight over this in Congress, it will bottleneck everything else, and we will still get no bill."[cxxi] Since Civil Rights clashes were rising within politics and on the streets, Robert Kennedy and Ted Sorenson advised that President Kennedy take more initiative in the legislative fight for equality.[cxxii] When Alabama Governor George Wallace decided to block two black students, Vivian Malone and James Hood, from entering and attending the University of Alabama on 11 June 1963, President Kennedy intervened with a firm hand. Wallace moved out of the way only when confronted by Deputy Attorney General Nicholas Katzenbach and the Alabama National Guard under orders from the president.

On that night, Kennedy provided his famous Civil Rights Address on national television and through the radio, which publicly launched his initiative for Civil Rights legislation that would provide equal access to public schools and other public places, along with greater protection for voting rights.[cxxiii] Kennedy's proposals helped create the Civil Rights Act of 1964, and that same day ended with the assassination of Medgar Evers, the NAACP leader, at his home in Mississippi.[cxxiv] The Southern Democrats and Republicans immediately reacted negatively to John F. Kennedy's speech, pushing down President Kennedy's efforts in Congress. When Arthur M. Schlesinger, Jr. praised Kennedy for his speech, the president replied, "Yes, and look at what happened to area development the very next day in the House…But of course, I had to give that speech, and I'm glad that I did."[cxxv] *The New York Times* published an article on 16 June comparing President Kennedy's previous reactions to how he functioned after his speech in regard to Civil Rights: before, the president "moved too slowly and with little evidence of deep moral commitment," but he "now demonstrates a genuine sense of urgency about eradicating racial discrimination from our national life."[cxxvi]

Despite Kennedy's efforts, the discrimination problem could not be solved so easily, and American citizens were displeased with the White House's progress. Over 100,000 protestors, which consisted mostly of black Americans, gathered in the nation's capital for the Civil Rights March on Washington for Jobs and Freedom on 28 August 1963. While Kennedy supported their efforts, he feared that the march would negatively affect the prospects for Civil Rights bills to pass through Congress; therefore, he declined an invitation to speak at the gathering. He was able, though, to give some of the details of the government's involvement to the Department of Justice, which channeled hundreds of thousands of dollars to the March's sponsors, two of them being the NAACP and MLK's Southern Christian Leadership Conference (SCLC).[cxxvii]

President Kennedy worked closely with the March organizers to ensure the demonstration would be peaceful. They personally edited speeches to remove inflammatory language and agreed the March would occur on a Wednesday and would end by four o'clock in the afternoon. Thousands of troops were on standby to make sure that the Protest would not grow violent. Afterward, the March was considered a "triumph of managed protest" as no demonstration-related arrests occurred. The president felt that the March was good for Civil Rights opportunities in the future and that it was a victory for him, bolstering chances to pass a Civil Rights bill.[cxxviii]

Just when things were looking up, the country experienced another setback. Three weeks after the March, a bomb exploded at the 16th Street Baptist Church in Birmingham on 15 September. Four black American children died in the explosion, and two other children were shot to death in the aftermath of the incident.[cxxix] In light of the violence, the Civil Rights legislation had to go through a few added amendments that hurt its chances of passing through Congress, which did not go over so well with JFK. He called the congressional leaders to the White House for a meeting, and the following day saw the original bill gain enough votes to pass through the House committee. Eventually, Kennedy's successor—Lyndon B. Johnson—enacted the legislation, which enforced voting rights, employment, education, public accommodations, and the administration of justice for all citizens of the United States.[cxxx]

Along with racial discrimination, President Kennedy also worked to tackle gender discrimination. On 14 December 1961, JFK signed the executive order that created the Presidential Commission on the Status of Women, a commission headed by former First lady Eleanor Roosevelt. The results revealed that, unsurprisingly, women had very different experiences than men within United States culture. The final Commission report, which was released in October 1963, documented legal and cultural barriers for women. On 10 June 1963, Kennedy signed the Equal Pay Act of 1963, which prohibited unequal payments based on gender, an amendment to the Fair Labor Standards Act.

Women and black Americans were not the only people Kennedy sought to assist during his administration. In his 1960 campaign, President Kennedy proposed a complete overhaul of America's policies on immigration and naturalization laws. He planned to ban discrimination on the basis of national origin, another hefty issue to take head-on. For President Kennedy, these ideas were simply an extension of his promise to ensure Civil Rights for Americans. His reforms to immigration policies became law with the Immigration and Nationality Act of 1965, which allowed the source of immigration in America to shift from European countries to Latin American and Asian nations. Policies also shifted to maintain a focus on unifying families, rather than specifically selecting individuals for immigration. JFK's brother, Senator Edward Kennedy, helped push the new legislation through the Senate.

Early in 1960, the country saw the conception of the Apollo Program under the Eisenhower administration as a follow-up to Project Mercury. The Apollo Program involved a shuttle that astronauts could use to orbit the Earth and attempt to land on the moon or, at least, orbit around it. NASA began planning for Apollo without definite funding under Eisenhower. As a United States Senator, Kennedy was opposed to the space program and desired its complete termination, but his ideas altered once in the presidency.[cxxxi]

While determining how to run his presidential administration, Kennedy chose to retain Eisenhower's science adviser, Jerome Wiesner, as the leader of the President's Science Advisory Committee.

During President Kennedy's State of the Union address in January 1961, he suggested the international community should cooperate in space exploration. Khrushchev declined, of course, because the Soviets did not wish to share their advancements in rocketry and space capabilities.[cxxxii] All of Kennedy's advisors told him any opportunities for space travel and exploration would be unnecessarily expensive, so the president was understandably nervous about the prospects. However, thanks to Lyndon B. Johnson, who supported the space program while in the Senate, Kennedy held off on his plans to dismantle the program.[cxxxiii]

President Kennedy's opinions on the space program changed on 12 April 1961 when Yuri Gagarin, a Soviet cosmonaut, became the first person to fly into space. This advancement increased American fears about being left behind the Soviet Union in regard to technological competition.[cxxxiv] Feeling the same sentiment as most of his people, President Kennedy grew eager for the United States to push by the Soviet Union to take the lead in what was dubbed the Space Race so that the country could maintain its strategy and prestige.

Kennedy sent a memo to Johnson on 20 April that asked him to look into the American space program and try to figure out how to help it catch up to the Soviet Union. Johnson checked with a few people whose judgment he trusted before replying a week later: "We are neither making maximum effort nor achieving results necessary if this country is to reach a position of leadership." Ted Sorensen told Kennedy that he should make great efforts in order to support the space program if it were to succeed in landing a person on the moon. On 25 May, Kennedy announced the lofty goal in his speech "Special Message to the Congress on Urgent National Needs":

"I believe that this nation should commit itself to achieving the goal, before this decade is out, of landing a man on the Moon and returning him safely to the Earth. No single space project in this period will be more impressive to mankind, or more important for the long-range exploration of space, and none will be so difficult or expensive to accomplish. We propose to accelerate the development of the appropriate lunar spacecraft. We propose to develop alternate liquid and solid fuel boosters, much larger than any now being developed, until certain which is superior. We propose additional funds for other engine development and for unmanned explorations—explorations which are particularly important for one purpose which this nation will never overlook: the survival of the man who first makes this daring flight. But in a very real sense, it will not be one man going to the moon—if we make this judgment affirmatively, it will be an entire nation. For all of us must work to put him there."

When Congress authorized the necessary funding, James E. Webb, the NASA administrator under President Kennedy, started the long process of reorganizing NASA though increasing the program's staffing level and building two new centers: a Launch Operations Center for the large moon rocket northwest of Cape Canaveral Air Force Station and a Manned Spacecraft Center on land that Rice University donated in Houston, Texas.

In light of Rice's donation, President Kennedy delivered a speech at their university on 12 September 1962 in an effort to promote the space program. He said:

"If this capsule history of our progress teaches us anything, it is that man, in his quest for knowledge and progress, is determined and cannot be deterred. The exploration of space will go ahead, whether we join in it or not, and it is one of the great adventures of all time, and no nation which expects to be the leader of other nations can expect to stay behind in this race for space.

Those who came before us made certain that this country rode the first waves of the industrial revolution, the first waves of modern invention, and the first wave of nuclear power and this generation does not intend to founder in the backwash of the coming age of space. We mean to be a part of it—we mean to lead it. For the eyes of the world now look into space, to the moon and to the planets beyond, and we have vowed that we shall not see it governed by a hostile flag of conquest, but by a banner of freedom and peace. We have vowed that we shall not see space filled with weapons of mass destruction, but with instruments of knowledge and understanding.

Yet the vows of this Nation can only be fulfilled if we in this Nation are first, and, therefore, we intend to be first. In short, our leadership in science and industry, our hopes for peace and security, our obligations to ourselves as well as others, all require us to make this effort, to solve these mysteries, to solve them for the good of all men, and to become the world's leading space-faring nation."

Kennedy was making an argument and formulating it well. He knew what he wanted for the United States and planned to deliver it. Almost six years after Kennedy's death, on 20 July 1969, Apollo 11 landed the first manned spacecraft on the Moon.

Chapter Nine: Assassination

Perhaps the most well-known fact about President John F. Kennedy is that he met an untimely end before his presidency was over. At 12:30 in the afternoon on Friday, 22 November 1963, President Kennedy was assassinated in Dallas, Texas, where he had traveled to attempt smoothing over frictions between two Democratic politicians in Texas. Kennedy was shot twice, once through the back and again in the head. America gasped loudly and wept for the young leader.

JFK was in a motorcade, sitting beside his wife in the back of an open car as they waved to the surrounding crowd. Soon after they turned a corner, two gunshots rang out over the crowd. People at the scene recall thinking that a motorcycle had backfired. When Jacqueline saw her husband slumped down beside her, she panicked, attempting to collect a piece of his skull that had become detached. Kennedy was rushed to Parkland Hospital for emergency medical treatment, but the surgeries were unsuccessful. The President of the United States died thirty minutes later. At the time of death, President Kennedy was 46 years old and had been serving as the president for a little over 1,000 days.

Lee Harvey Oswald was arrested for the murder, but denied shooting and claimed he was framed. Before he could be prosecuted for the shooting, he was killed by Jack Ruby on 24 November. Ruby was arrested and convicted of Oswald's murder, but he successfully appealed his conviction only to die of cancer on 3 January 1967, before he could attend his new trial.

Lyndon B. Johnson was quickly sworn into office while Jacqueline Kennedy stood next to him. Through an executive order, he created the Warren Commission, which was under the control of Chief Justice Earl Warren. The sole purpose of the Commission was to investigate the assassination. In conclusion, they determined that Oswald acted alone in the murder and was part of no external or internal conspiracy.

America was feeling the effect of the assassination, and political repercussions were apparent. Even as late as 2004, a news poll showed that 66% of responding Americans thought the assassination was part of a larger conspiracy, and 74% thought there had been a cover-up in the government. In 1979, the United States House Select Committee on Assassinations said it thought "that Kennedy was probably assassinated as a result of a conspiracy. The committee was unable to identify the other gunmen or the extent of the conspiracy." Historian Carl M. Brauer argued in 2002 that the public's "fascination with the assassination may indicate a psychological denial of John F. Kennedy's death, a mass wish to…undo it."[cxxxv]

The Cathedral of St. Matthew of the Apostle held a Requiem mass for Kennedy on 25 November 1963. Father John J. Cavanaugh officiated the ceremony. Later, both of JFK's brothers—Robert and Ted Kennedy—had funerals modeled after his own. After the funeral, the president was buried in a small plot within Arlington National Cemetery. Over the next three years, it is estimated that 16 million people visited his grave to pay their respects. According to testimonies, "Alan Seeger's 'I Have a Rendezvous with Death' was one of John F. Kennedy's favorite poems and he often asked his wife to recite it." Unfortunately, Kennedy's meeting with Death came a little too soon in life.

It was only a short while after John F. Kennedy's death that his presidency came to be known as the Camelot Era. Only a week later, Jacqueline Kennedy said in a *Life* magazine interview with Theodore H. White: "Don't let it be forgot, that there was a spot, for one brief shining moment that was known as Camelot. There'll be great presidents again, but there will never be another Camelot."

JFK's assassination not only had a dreadful effect on the nation in regard to the people's safety consciousness, but it also affected other parts of society in less obvious ways. Kennedy, of course, was the first president to heavily utilize television for political gain. His death greatly showcased that fact. Coverage of his death was mostly given through television. Newspaper clippings of headlines on the assassination were kept as souvenirs rather than sources of the latest information. At the time of his death, all three major United States television networks suspended their scheduled timeslots to cover the death. For 70 hours, nothing was on television except for news of the assassination, which made this coverage the longest uninterrupted news story on American television until 9/11.

Just as people do now with 9/11 memories, people alive during the John F. Kennedy assassination recall where they were when they heard the news that he had been shot in Dallas. The United Nations Ambassador Adlai Stevenson said, "All of us…will bear the grief of his death until the day of ours." Even people who were not alive during the assassination are heavily affected by Kennedy's death. Conspiracy theorists still gather to discuss how Kennedy may have been involved in something about which no one knew, something no one was supposed to know.

Chapter Ten: Legacy

Decades after his death, people recall John F. Kennedy as a kind president who tried his best to do what he could to improve the lives of the American people. His funeral was a momentous event, bringing in representatives from over 90 countries. Specific groups of people recalled his influence on them, as well. The United States Special Forces reverently regarded their relationship with Kennedy. Forrest Lindley who wrote for the United States military newspaper *Stars and Stripes* said, "It was President Kennedy who was responsible for the rebuilding of the Special Forces and giving us back our Green Beret." Kennedy was the first of six presidents to have served in the United States Navy, as well, and one of his most noticeable contributions to the administration was his support of the creation of the Navy SEALs in 1961.[cxxxvi]

President Kennedy pushed the country toward what is possibly the most important turn in American history: the institution of the Civil Rights Act of 1964, which eventually ended the reign of racist terror in the "Solid South." He provided economic aid to South Vietnam, delivered iconic speeches, and inspired Americans to be better. President Kennedy successfully pushed America forward in the Space Race, curtailing Soviet efforts to rise above. After JFK's death, he was given the *Pacem in Terris* (Peace on Earth) Award. Needless to say, Kennedy's legacy will live on long after today. Although he was only in office for a short period of time, he is often voted as one of America's best presidents, alongside Abraham Lincoln, George Washington, and Franklin D. Roosevelt.

Help Requested

If you enjoyed this particular part on John F Kennedy, then it would be really appreciated it if you would post a short review for the book on Amazon.

Thanks for your support!

Part 2: Jackie Kennedy

A Captivating Guide to the Life of Jacqueline Kennedy Onassis

Introduction

Without a doubt, the name *Jackie Kennedy* draws multiple thoughts to mind; she is, perhaps, most well-known in her service as the first lady of the United States, as her husband, John F. Kennedy, took office as the president, and her role in restoring the White House. Then, of course, other people remember Jacqueline for her role in the fashion industry, particularly her pink Chanel suit and matching pillbox hat, which became a symbol of her husband's assassination. Jackie is so renowned and beloved that she ranks as one of the most popular first ladies. In fact, Jacqueline was named in 1999 on Gallup's list of Most Admired Men and Women in twentieth-century America. While she made major impacts on the White House, Jackie was much more than her title as first lady.

First of all, she was a mother. Not only that, but she was also a mother in the spotlight in the 1960s. People rushed to ask Jacqueline about her ideas on various parts of motherhood and her position as a wife in the White House. In reality, the family was privileged but not that much different from others of their wealth level. Later, her son said, "It's hard to talk about a legacy or a mystique. It's my family. It's my mother. It's my sister. It's my father. We're a family like any other. We look out for one another. The fact that there have been difficulties and hardships, or obstacles, makes us closer."[cxxxvii]

Jackie held a tight grip on her role in her personal life and government. John F. Kennedy goes as far as to say that his wife was the reason he won re-election to Senate. She was somehow both charismatic and shy, appealing to a broad range of the public. Historian Arthur M.

Schlesinger visited the Kennedy Compound in Hyannis Port in July 1959 and said that he found Jacqueline to have "tremendous awareness, an all-seeing eye, and a ruthless judgment."[cxxxviii]

Jackie kept people on the edge, and the media never quite knew what to expect from her both within her husband's presidency and removed from it. She was quite the polar opposite of first ladies Eleanor Roosevelt and Hillary Rodham Clinton when it came to involvement in her husband's presidency and policies. In fact, she baffled news reporters when she admitted that she did not even know the date of her husband's inauguration. Jacqueline replied "Acapulco" when asked what she thought would be a suitable venue for the next Democratic convention. This part of her personality was probably due to her dislike of the media, though. She felt no need to parade her knowledge or her family in front of the cameras and often chose to stand to the side instead of engaging, whereas her husband loved interacting with the press and did so much more often than she would have liked.

Although she seemed a bit out of the loop at times, Jackie was not ditsy or clueless about her husband's responsibilities in the political realm. Rather, she was a first lady at a point in time when many American citizens did not appreciate the idea of a president's wife being too involved in his politics and policies. The more people actually study this particular first lady, though, the more the American public knows about her real place in the White House. Like many wives of presidential marriages, Jacqueline appeared to have little to no influence on the presidency, but she held a good bit of power beneath the surface. In fact, the Kennedy Library holds the first lady's oral history, which displays her opinions of everyone within John F. Kennedy's administration, ideas which she clearly shared with her husband. The people she praised in her oral history tended to gain promotion under President Kennedy, and those she disliked did not gain much ground within the White House.

For the most part, Jacqueline was a strong force her entire life, including her time in the White House. She swept the public and the media off their feet with her fashion choices and her personality, and she warmed the White House with her care for its people and its structural integrity, alongside its function as a home for her children. In all, Jacqueline's contributions to the United States are not to be underestimated.

Chapter One: Childhood and Early Education

On July 28, 1929, Jackie was born as Jacqueline Lee Bouvier in Southampton, New York, in Southampton Hospital. Her mother was Janet Norton Lee (1907 –1989), and her father was John Vernou "Black Jack" Bouvier III (1891 – 1957). Janet Norton Lee's ancestry was of Irish descent, while John Vernou Bouvier III's family hailed from France, Scotland, and England. Soon after her birth, Jacqueline was baptized at the Church of St. Ignatius Loyola in Manhattan. A few years later in 1933, the Bouvier family welcomed a new member, Caroline Lee Bouvier, who would later be Caroline Lee Radziwill-Ross. Both sisters were reared strictly in the Catholic faith.

As a young child, Jackie was establishing her independence and quick wit, and it was noticeable to everyone who interacted with her. While on a walk with her nanny and little sister, Jackie wandered away from the small group. When a police officer stopped her, worried about a young girl alone, she told him, "My nurse and baby sister seem to be lost," effectively displaying that she did not blame herself for the situation.[cxxxix] Her take-control attitude followed her throughout her entire life.

Jacqueline spent much of her early childhood between Manhattan and Lasata, which was the Bouviers' country estate in East Hampton on Long Island. She and her father formed a very close relationship that often excluded her sister, Lee, much to the younger sister's disappointment. John Vernou Bouvier III claimed that Jackie was the "most beautiful daughter a man ever had."[cxl]

In her childhood, Jacqueline dabbled in multiple hobbies, as many children do. She exceeded all expectations with her mastery of horseback-riding. In fact, her mother placed her on a horse when she was only one year old. By the time Jackie turned twelve years old, she had a few national championships under her belt. In 1940, *The New York Times* wrote, "Jacqueline Bouvier, an eleven-year-old equestrienne from Easy Hampton, Long Island, scored a double victory in the horsemanship competition. Miss Bouvier achieved a rare distinction. The occasions are few when a young rider wins both contests in the same show."[cxli] She continued to compete successfully in the sport and lived on as an avid equestrienne for the rest of her life.[cxlii]

She did not stop her hobbies at horseback-riding. Additionally, Jackie spent long hours buried in books, took ballet lessons, and developed a passion for learning languages. French was a particular favorite and was emphasized in her childhood education.[cxliii] These developed language skills helped Jacqueline as she entered her husband's political realm. Whereas John F. Kennedy often needed a translator in foreign countries and with foreign dignitaries, his wife could often speak their language fluently.

Before she even began school, young Jackie read all the books on her bookshelves. She loved Mowgli from Rudyard Kipling's *The Jungle Book*, Little Lord Fauntleroy's grandfather, Robin Hood, Scarlett O'Hara from *Gone with the Wind*, and the poetry of Lord Byron. Her mother often wondered if she would one day make a career of writing.[cxliv] Near a childhood Christmas, she penned the following poem:

"Christmas is coming

Santa Claus is near

Reindeer hooves will soon be drumming

On the roof tops loud and clear."[cxlv]

Referring to reading as a child, Jackie said, "I lived in New York City until I was thirteen and spent the summers in the country. I hated dolls, loved horses and dogs, and had skinned knees and braces on my teeth for what must have seemed an interminable length of time to my family. I read a lot when I was little, much of which was too old for me. There were Chekhov and Shaw in the room where I had to take naps and I never slept but sat on the windowsill reading, then scrubbed the soles of my feet so the nurse would not see I had been out of bed."[cxlvi] Jacqueline had a thirst for learning, and she never quite quenched it.

After attending kindergarten, Jackie enrolled in Manhattan's Chapin School in 1935. The Chapin School, an all-girls independent day school, presented a space for young Jackie to learn everything she needed to know from grades one to six.[cxlvii] Although she was quite smart, Jackie often found herself in trouble at school. Her teacher said that she was "a darling child, the prettiest little girl, very clever, very artistic, and full of the devil."[cxlviii] She was a very mischievous child and found herself sent to the headmistress, Miss Ethel Stringfellow, many times. Stringfellow wrote on Jacqueline's report card: "Jacqueline was given a D in Form because her disturbing conduct in her geography class made it necessary to exclude her from the room."[cxlix] Like most parents, Jackie's mother made excuses for her daughter's actions, saying that Jackie finished assignments early and acted out in boredom.[cl] Janet Bouvier once asked her daughter, "What happens when you're sent to Miss Stringfellow?" Young Jackie replied, "Well, I go to the office and Miss Stringfellow says, 'Jacqueline, sit down. I've heard bad reports about you.' I sit down. Then Miss Stringfellow says a lot of things—but I don't listen." Cool and calm, she was unwilling to admit guilt.

Biographer Sarah Bradford says, "Jackie was already a rebel, unsubdued by the discipline at Miss Chapin's. She was brighter than most of her classmates and would get through her work quickly, then was left with nothing to do but doodle and daydream. All the teachers interviewed by Mary Van Rensselaer Thayer twenty years later remembered her for her beauty and, above all, her mischief."[cli] Even then, Jackie was creating a name for herself. She would not be forgotten easily.

Nothing in Jackie's life was smooth. Jacqueline's father had a reputation for cheating on his wife and partaking in too much liquor too fast. By the time young Jackie was born, John Bouvier was involved in several affairs already. Jackie's mother attempted to give the marriage another chance, encouraging her husband to focus on his job as a stockbroker, which had thus far produced no positive results.[clii] She grew embittered with her husband and quickly realized she wanted out of the marriage. She still had her children to consider, though. It bothered Janet Bouvier to no end that her children obviously preferred their father's company over hers. She had a tendency to overreact to situations and occasionally hit her girls, which only made them prefer their father even more.

In a 2013 interview, Lee, Jackie's sister, said that her mother was too concerned with her "almost irrational social climbing," but when referring to her father she said, "He was a wonderful man … He had such funny idiosyncrasies, like always wearing his black patent evening shoes with his swimming trunks. One thing which infuriates me is how he's always labeled the drunk black prince. He was never drunk with me, though I'm sure he sometimes drank, due to my mother's constant nagging. You would, and I would."[cliii]

During Jacqueline's time at the Chapin School, her parents were experiencing another bout of marital issues. On top of her father's extramarital affairs, he was also an alcoholic. To boot, the family drowned in financial instability after Wall Street crashed in 1929. Although her father built some of the most distinguished apartments on Park Avenue in New York, his loss of money was excessive. He made too many bad investments and did not spend well, in general. Jacqueline later said that she was afraid that her father would not be able to pay her tuition to school.

In 1936, Jacqueline's parents separated and were granted a divorce four years later. Janet Bouvier hoped that the time apart—the separation—would show her husband that he needed to learn family responsibility. During their separation, the press published all the gory and intimate details of their personal lives. Detailed photographs showed evidence of John Bouvier's dalliances, which embarrassed his wife no end.[cliv] Lee said, "There was such relentless bitterness on both sides. Jackie was really fortunate to have or acquire the ability to tune out, which she always kept ... It was like for the years from ten to twenty never hearing anything [from your parents] except how awful the other one was."[clv]

Apparently, Jackie learned at a very young age how to conceal her true feelings. Her cousin John H. Davis said that she had a "tendency to withdraw frequently into a private world of her own."[clvi] Although she was able to restrain her opinions as a younger woman and child, the truth of it all came out later: she was deeply affected by the divorce and the media attention that came along with it. For the rest of her life, Jackie would hate the press and would try at all costs to control the narrative they were printing. Often, she would seek journalists who would print what she wanted, such as Theodore White, the man who printed her story of Camelot she invented the week after her husband's assassination.

Jacqueline's mother remarried later to Hugh Dudley Auchincloss, Jr., the heir of Standard Oil.[clvii] The Bouvier sisters had three new stepsiblings from the wedding, offspring of Auchincloss' previous two marriages. Additionally, Jacqueline's mother and Auchincloss had two more children together.

After the marriage, the Bouvier sisters moved their primary residence to Auchincloss' Merrywood estate in McLean, Virginia. They also spent a good deal of time at their new stepfather's other estate, Hammersmith Farm, in Newport, Rhode Island, and in their father's homes in Long Island and New York City. Jackie began to see her stepfather as a source of stability; he was able to provide monetary funding and a pampered childhood, which her father could never do on quite as grand a scale. Although Jacqueline felt at home with her new family, she was a bit of an outcast within their new social circle. Many of her new family's friends were white Anglo-Saxon protestants (WASPS), and her position as a Catholic left her as an outsider with her religion and her status as a child of divorce, which was an uncommon trait in the elite social group.[clviii]

Jacqueline grew very fond of her stepfather, regardless of the issues of social anxiety and distance. At the age of twenty-three, she wrote a series of poems that highlighted things in her life made possible by her mother's marriage to Auchincloss. In an introduction, she wrote: "It seems so hard to believe that you've been married ten years. I think they must have been the very best decade of your lives. At the start, in 1942, we all had other lives and we were seven people thrown together, so many little separate units that could have stayed that way. Now we are nine—and what you've given us and what we've shared has bound us all to each other for the rest of our lives."[clix] Jacqueline truly appreciated the stability granted to her by her mother's divorce.

When Jackie finished six years at the Chapin School, she moved on to the Holton-Arms School in Northwest Washington, D.C., which she attended from 1942 to 1944. Here, she grew fond of Miss Helen Shearman, the Latin teacher. She claimed that the instructor was demanding, "But she was right. We were all lazy teenagers. Everything she taught me stuck, and though I hated to admit it, I adored Latin."[clx]

Jacqueline transferred to Miss Porter's School, a boarding school for girls in Farmington, Connecticut, attending from 1944 to 1947. Along with a rigorous academic schedule, the school emphasized proper manners and the art of conversation. At Miss Porter's Jacqueline felt she could distance herself from her mother's new family, allowing her to pursue independence and college preparatory classes.[clxi] Here, she began learning to function on her own, something she would have to do at various points in her life whether she wanted to do so or not.

Jackie did well at Miss Porter's School. Upon graduation, Jacqueline was listed as one of the top students of her class; she received the Maria McKinney Memorial Award for Excellence in Literature.[clxii] Her senior class yearbook claimed that she was known for "her wit, her accomplishment as a horsewoman, and her unwillingness to become a housewife." She even wrote in the class yearbook under the *Ambition in Life* section: "Not to be a housewife," but Jacqueline grew worried about her future prospects eventually.[clxiii] She later wrote to a friend: "I just know no one will ever marry me and I'll end up as a house mother at Farmington."[clxiv]

Chapter Two: College and Early Career

After finishing her career in early education, Jacqueline enrolled in Vassar College in Poughkeepsie, New York. Here, she gained a good bit of notoriety. She had preferred to attend Sarah Lawrence College, but her parents forbade her to do so. Therefore, she avoided the social life at Vassar, but she participated heavily in the art and drama clubs and wrote for the newspaper at the college.[clxv]

Rather than remaining active with her classmates, she returned to Manhattan on the weekends. Before entering college, Jacqueline was introduced into society, and her face henceforth became a common feature in New York social functions. In fact, columnist Igor Cassini called her the "debutante of the year" after her formal "coming out" party, a title which she tried not to carry around with her.[clxvi] Charlotte Curtis, Jackie's next-door neighbor in the Main Hall, said, "I knew about her Deb of the Year title, but I don't remember her ever bringing it up. I think it rather embarrassed her." Curtis' roommate said that Jacqueline was:

"intellectually very curious. She constantly asked me about my family. I was of Lebanese extraction and had grown up in a small town in Tennessee. These aspects of my life fascinated Jackie. She wanted to know all about how my father stowed away on a boat as a young boy to come to America She wanted to know about Lebanon. I had pictures of my family in my room and Jackie would scrutinize the faces and ask questions about various members of the family, almost like a reporter gathering material for a story. She had a way of focusing on a person that left one dazzled. It was most flattering."

It seems that even this early in life, Jacqueline was learning to make others love and care for her the same way she did for them. She was learning how to charm the pants off people, and it was working.

At this point in her life, Jacqueline began dating, as well. She entered that confusing realm of college dating and completely took control of it. Her title of "Debutante of the Year" had suitors lining up at her door even as her stepbrother, Yusha, who was an upperclassman at Yale, was setting her up with friends from Ivy League schools. More than anything else, she was testing the water. Later, her stepbrother said, "It was a transitory period of her life. She liked playing the field, meeting a variety of types—varsity swimmers at Yale, Harvard pre-med candidates, up-and-coming New York lawyers and stockbrokers." She took none of these men seriously and referred to them as "beetle-browed bores."[clxvii] She made it quite obvious that she just wanted to have a fun time.

Although she learned a lot at the school, Jackie spent as much time away from Vassar as possible. Wishing to engage in a study-abroad experience, she spent her junior year of college in France at the University of Grenoble and at the Sorbonne in Paris. Here, she lived with the well-to-do de Renty family at 76 Avenue Mozart. She vacationed with Claude de Renty, daughter of her landlady, while living in Paris and wrote of the trip they took together in 1950: "I had the most terrific vacation in Austria and Germany. We really saw what it was like with the Russians with Tommy guns in Vienna. We saw Vienna and Salzburg and Berchtesgaden where Hitler lived: Munich and the Dachau concentration camp ... It's so much more fun traveling second and third class and sitting up all night in trains, as you really get to know people and hear their stories. When I traveled before it was all too luxurious and we didn't see anything."[clxviii] During the trip, they spent a good bit of time in southern France, a place Jacqueline came to love dearly:

"I just can't tell you what it is like to come down from the mountains of Grenoble to this flat, blazing plain where seven-eighths of all you see is hot blue sky—and there are rows of poplars at the edge of every field to protect the crops from the mistral and spiky short palm trees with blazing red flowers growing at their feet. The people here speak with the lovely twang of the 'accent du Midi.' They are always happy as they live in the sun and love to laugh. It was heartbreaking to only get such a short glimpse of it all—I want to go back and soak it all up. The part I want to see is la Camargue—a land in the Rhone delta which is flooded by the sea every year and they have a ceremony where they all wade in on horses and bless it—La Bénédiction de la Mer—gypsies live there and bands of little Arab horses and they raise wild bulls."[clxix]

Jackie relished her time abroad. Later, she wrote: "I loved it more than any year of my life. Being away from home gave me a chance to look at myself with a jaundiced eye. I learned not to be ashamed of a real hunger for knowledge, something I had always tried to hide, and I came home glad to start in here again but with a love for Europe that I am afraid will never leave me."[clxx] Her family still thought of her while she was gone, especially her very protective mother. Jacqueline once told her stepbrother, Hugh Auchincloss, "I have to write Mummy a ream each week or she gets hysterical and thinks I'm dead or married to an Italian."[clxxi] Near the end of her stint in France, Jackie's reputation was that of a society party girl. She attended countless parties overseas, much to the chagrin of her father who thought that her reputation was growing ill. He tried to convince her time and time again to stay away from men and to return home to him where he could protect her.

When she returned to the United States, she spent some time at Smith College in Massachusetts, then transferred to George Washington University in Washington, D.C. Jacqueline graduated with a Bachelor of Arts degree in French literature in 1951 with distinction and honors, never having lost her love of education; early in her marriage to Kennedy, she continued to take courses in American history at Georgetown University in Washington, D.C.

While attending George Washington University, Jacqueline won a twelve-month junior editorship at *Vogue* magazine in which she continued her passion for writing that she developed and fed at Vassar. In this coveted position, she was to work in the magazine's New York City office for six months and spend the rest of the time in Paris.^{clxxii} She never reached fruition in this editorship, though. On the first day of her job, the managing editor suggested that she leave the job and return to Washington, D.C. At the age of twenty-two, Jackie was beyond the appropriate age for a woman of her status to marry, and the editor was worried that the job would hinder her social position. Jackie followed the advice and returned home after only one day with *Vogue*.^{clxxiii}

Soon afterward, Jacqueline found a job as a part-time receptionist at the *Washington Times-Herald*. Although her mother was married to the heir of Standard Oil, his money did not extend heavily to Jackie and her sister. Therefore, her job was not only for experience but also from her need for a salary to support herself and her spending habits. She quickly grew bored with her position and approached the editor, Frank Waldrop, to ask for harder work. After much back-and-forth arguing, he agreed to give her a new position.

Jacqueline began functioning as the *Inquiring Camera Girl*. In this position, she popped smart, witty questions to random people on the street, took their pictures, and wrote a short snippet about their responses to be published alongside their pictures in the newspaper.^{clxxiv} Additionally, she wrote some of the included interest pieces. Jacqueline particularly enjoyed interviewing children, saying that "they make the best stories."^{clxxv} One of her interviewees was Tricia Nixon, daughter of Richard Nixon, who she interviewed a few days after her father took the vice presidency in the 1952 election. Her question was, "What do you think of Senator Nixon now?"^{clxxvi} Jacqueline was ecstatic for her work. She wrote to newspaperwoman Bess Furman: "I'm so in love with all that world now—I think I look up to newspaper people the way you join movie star fan clubs when you're ten years old."[clxxvii]

While Jacqueline was working for the *Washington Times-Herald*, she was briefly engaged to John G. W. Husted, Jr. A lot of fuzzy details surround this time. Since Jacqueline was such a private woman, it is unclear as to how the relationship began or ended or what happened between those times. She accepted his proposal around Christmas of 1951. Many people think they dated only a month before publishing the announcement of their engagement in *The New York Times* in January 1952. After three months, Jackie changed her mind, determining that Husted was "immature and boring."[clxxviii] He came to visit her at Merrywood, and Jacqueline placed her engagement ring in the pocket of his suit jacket when she dropped him off at the airport. Husted recalls, "She didn't say much and neither did I. There wasn't much you could say."[clxxix]

Chapter Three: Relationship with John F. Kennedy

In May 1952, journalist Charles L. Barlett introduced United States Representative John F. Kennedy to then Jacqueline Lee Bouvier at a dinner party. The two hit it off but did not really engage with one another until the next time they met. They found similarities in their religion, their loving relationships with reading, and their experiences abroad. They started dating around May 8, 1952 after another dinner at Charlie Bartlett's house. At the time, Kennedy was running for the United States Senate. Kennedy and Bouvier, later Kennedy Onassis, bonded heavily during this time and grew more serious after the November election.

Senator John F. Kennedy took Jacqueline Lee Bouvier to the President and the First Lady's Inaugural Ball on January 20, 1953, formally presenting their status as a couple to the public and to all of his political friends. Their relationship grew stronger and stronger, and Bouvier began searching for ways to introduce the Senator to her family. She arranged a date for her suitor to meet her father who was living in New York at the time. Soon after, Kennedy proposed to her, but Bouvier waited a short bit to accept. She was determined to remain devoted to reporting on the coronation of Queen Elizabeth II, her biggest job yet at the paper; therefore, she traveled to London for *The Washington Times-Herald* and didn't accept the marriage proposal until returning to the United States after a month in Europe. Upon her arrival, Kennedy slipped a two-carat diamond and emerald engagement ring on her finger, and she agreed to the marriage proposal. On June 25, 1953, the engagement was officially announced: "Senator Kennedy to marry in fall, son of former envoy is fiancée of Miss Jacqueline Bouvier, Newport Society Girl." [clxxx] After claiming acceptance, she resigned from her position at the newspaper.[clxxxi] She officially devoted herself to her husband's political campaigns, spending all of her time in this manner.

The Kennedys married in St. Mary's Church in Newport, Rhode Island, on September 12, 1953 during a mass led by Boston's Archbishop Richard Cushing.[clxxxii] Considered the largest social event of the season, the wedding had somewhere around seven hundred guests at the ceremony and upwards of three thousand at the following reception held at Hammersmith Farm. After the wedding, the couple spent a honeymoon in Acapulco, Mexico, before returning to their new home, dubbed Hickory Hill, in McLean, Virginia, which was conveniently close to Washington, D.C. Here, Jacqueline spent long hours reading congressional records in an attempt to familiarize herself with her husband's work so that she could provide as much assistance as possible.[clxxxiii] Additionally, she enrolled in an American History course at the School of Foreign Service at Georgetown University.

Their marriage was not a particularly easy one. As early as two weeks into their marriage, JFK was looking for ways to be with other women. Margaret Coit, winner of a Pulitzer Prize, admitted in 1966, "I had designs on John F. Kennedy. Everybody in Massachusetts did. He was the golden boy, the most eligible bachelor in new England." Coit was only one of the many women who have admitted to having been involved with the president in some way or another. All the Secret Service agents were, of course, privy to the comings and goings of his suitors after he became president of the United States, and it is thought that Jackie had a few affairs of her own, though none so overt as President Kennedy's dalliances. Thankfully and tragically, Jackie was accustomed to men who prowled, being her father's daughter.

According to most records, she did not think much about her husband's infidelity. She had other things to occupy her mind.

Furthermore, President John F. Kennedy suffered from Addison's disease in addition to his chronic back pain left over from a war injury. He underwent two spinal surgeries in late 1954, and each was near fatal.[clxxxiv] It got to the point where a priest was summoned to administer the last rites to Senator Kennedy. Jacqueline sat by her husband the entire time, holding his hands and keeping him up to date on what was happening in the news.[clxxxv] She was nothing if not the perfect future first lady. JFK began to show signs of recovery and was discharged from the New York hospital. He spent the next while in Palm Beach, Florida, and had a second operation on February 15, 1955.[clxxxvi]

On top of all these difficulties, the couple experienced trouble having children; Jacqueline had a miscarriage in 1955 and gave birth to a stillborn daughter in August 1956. Finally, Jackie gave birth to Caroline on November 27, 1957 after a grueling Caesarean section. With their new daughter, the couple posed proudly for the cover of the April 21, 1958 issue of *Life*.

Around this time, JFK was campaigning for re-election to the Senate. Jacqueline went anywhere her husband did. By Kennedy's side at many rallies stood his wife and daughter, and he soon began to realize that Jacqueline added positive value to the campaign trail. American political consultant Kenneth O'Donnell said that Jacqueline's presence meant that "the size of the crowd was twice as big," and she was "always cheerful and obliging." When JFK gained re-election to a second term in November 1958, he credited his wife's visibility. In his words, she was "simply invaluable."[clxxxvii]

During that year, JFK traveled across fourteen states. Jacqueline and Caroline were sometimes in attendance, and sometimes they were on long breaks away from the political realm. Regardless of where Jackie happened to be physically, she provided invaluable support to her husband in preparation for his intended presidential campaign. For example, to help Kennedy garner Louisiana's support, she traveled to the state to visit Edmund Reggie, an American Democratic politician who served as a city judge in Louisiana.

Chapter Four: Motherhood

Although Jacqueline would have healthy children, her luck was not always with her. On August 23, 1956, Jacqueline gave birth to a stillborn child, which she named Arabella. Those around her say she handled it calmly and did not ask her husband to return from his cruise in the Mediterranean. She had almost recovered from her melancholy when she was further saddened by her father's death on August 3, 1957. Although he was a troublesome father, they still had a good relationship. Jacqueline immediately went to him and planned his funeral, herself. She still had motherhood in the back of her mind, though.

Her luck began to look up when she gave birth to a daughter named Caroline Bouvier Kennedy on the eve of Thanksgiving Day, November 27, 1957. Archbishop Cushing baptized the new Kennedy baby on December 13, 1957. The paparazzi were somewhat interested in the Kennedy family at this point, and Jackie was annoyed with them and their insistent meddling: "Nothing disturbs me as much as interviews and journalists. That's the trouble with life in the public eye. I have always hated gossip-columnists, publicity about the private lives of public men. But if you make your living in public office, you're the property of every taxpaying citizen. Your whole life is an open book."[clxxxviii]

John F. Kennedy defeated Richard Nixon, his Republican opponent, on November 8, 1960, thus becoming the new president-elect. Two weeks later, Jacqueline gave birth to John F. Kennedy, Jr., in a Caesarean section on November 25, 1960. The next two weeks she spent in the hospital, and she was watched carefully by the media. The birth turned out to be the Kennedy family's first bout of national media attention. While they told the press that the mother and child were happy and healthy, their son was actually suffering from an undiagnosed respiratory ailment. He spent the first six days of his life in an incubator, and it took months for them both to recover from the ordeal.[clxxxix] When JFK saw his son, he said, "Now, that's the most beautiful boy I've seen. Maybe I'll name him Abraham Lincoln."[cxc] When asked what he planned for his son, Kennedy answered that he wanted young John to enter politics because it was a fulfilling place, but he quickly followed with "I want him to do whatever makes him happy—whatever that is."[cxci]

Jacqueline spent two weeks after her son's birth in bed, and her son was not faring too well, either. He was rapidly losing weight, crying nonstop, and struggling to breathe. Later, they discovered he was suffering from the same illness that killed his younger brother. She later said, "John's health really wasn't doing so well. There was, thank God, this brilliant pediatrician in Palm Beach who really saved his life, as he was going downhill."[cxcii] To satisfy their daughter, the Kennedys told her that the baby was her birthday present, as he was born only two days before she turned three. Caroline fell in love with her new brother and believed that he was a splendid present. In fact, the children's nanny said that "Caroline thought for a long time that he belonged to her."[cxciii]

Jackie became pregnant again in 1963, which led her to step away from her duties as first lady. Five weeks ahead of her due date, she went into labor on August 7, 1963, giving birth to Patrick Bouvier Kennedy in an emergency Caesarean section at Otis Air Force Base. At birth, his lungs were not fully developed, so he was quickly transferred from Cape Cod to Boston Children's Hospital. Two days after she gave birth, he died from hyaline membrane disease, which is a syndrome in premature infants when they develop lungs that are structurally immature.[cxciv] While Jacqueline remained at Otis Air Force

Base to recuperate, JFK traveled to Boston to be with their son and was there at his death. On August 14, 1963, he returned to take his wife home.

Soon after her son's death, Jackie entered a deep depression. She had experienced a great deal of grief already in the past few years, and this tragedy tipped her over the edge. Interestingly enough, the death brought the Kennedy couple closer in their grief. According to Arthur Schlesinger, Kennedy always "regarded Jacqueline with genuine affection and pride," but their marriage "never seemed more solid than in the later months of 1963."[cxcv]

Kennedy began to think that his wife may need a little time away from the White House and looked for vacation options. It was soon after her child's death that Jacqueline joined Aristotle Onassis, the man who would later be her second husband, on a yacht trip. Jacqueline's sister, connected them together. President Kennedy was wary but thought that time away would be "good for her." The general public and many people within the Kennedy administration deeply disapproved of this time away from the White House. When the first lady returned, she said she regretted being away for so long but said she was "melancholy about the death of [her] baby."[cxcvi]

Jackie did not let anything come between her and the future well-being of her children. In his book *The Good Son: JFK Jr. and the Mother He Loved,* Christopher Andersen tells a story of how Jacqueline was watching out for her children even in her most grievous moment: "With her eye undoubtedly on John's future, Jackie bent down and instructed the three-year-old to deliver history's most famous salute as his father's horse-drawn casket passed before him—in that moment securing his place forever in the national consciousness."[cxcvii] She kept her concern close to her heart, only intervening in her children's lives when she deemed it necessary.

It is too easy to forget that Jackie was not only the president's wife but that she was also a mother. In fact, she held a few groundbreaking ideas on parenting. Pamela Keogh, author of *Jackie Style*, describes Jacqueline as an "extremely hands-on, very involved" mother, especially for her class position. Often, wealthy women left their children with a nanny all the time and thought nothing of it. Keogh tells *People Magazine* that "Jackie was—there" for Caroline and John Jr., her two children. "She was there playing with them and reading to them and painting with them—all kinds of stuff. She was a young mother but she wasn't phoning it in, and she was very involved. That's why her two children were beautifully raised."[cxcviii] Keogh says that although the family kept a nanny, Maud Shaw, Jacqueline was always there to oversee everything that happened. Jackie said, "I'll be a wife and mother first, then first lady."[cxcix] She allowed her children to have independence. She wanted them to forge their own paths, taking risks and making their own decisions, but she wanted to be there every step of the way in case they needed her for anything.

The children, of course, had every luxury they could imagine while living at the White House, but Jacqueline thought it was important that her children remained "modest, humble, and down-to-earth … They had to pick up their own clothing. She made sure that the Secret Service agents were not maids. The Secret Service agents could not fetch the children anything."[cc] She tried to make the White House as close to a normal house as she possibly could. Jacqueline said, "If Jack proved to be the greatest president of the century and his children turned out badly, it would be a tragedy."[cci]

Jacqueline's former Secret Service agent Clint Hill recalls that the Kennedy parents "insisted on their children being respectful, acknowledging people and having good manners … but at the same time they wanted them to have a lot of fun and be happy."[ccii] Former Secret Service agent Tom Wells told *People Magazine*, "When [the Kennedy children] were at the White House, there was a privilege involved there but still they weren't isolated … Ms. Shaw used to take them to the park to meet their friends. They went to other friends' houses from time to time, and their friends would also come to the

White House. They were engaged in lots of activities."[cciii] Keogh says that Jackie wanted to help her children gain independence, even in their intense privilege: "If they got themselves into a scrape, they had to get themselves out of it."

Additionally, Jackie acted as the disciplinarian in the family since she spent the largest amount of time with her children. Keogh says, "Jackie ran a tight ship ... She checked the homework and she made sure they were dressed properly. If John was acting up, she made him go stand in a corner. It wasn't a tough house, but there were expectations."[cciv] Jackie was also a playful mother, though. She attempted to teach her children about all of her favorite hobbies, encouraging them to pursue things that made them happy and brought them joy. "She was fun," said Keogh. "You can see the pictures. She was running with the kids and playing with them." Clint Hill said Jacqueline particularly enjoyed trying to teach Caroline to ride horses. In 1962, Jacqueline had a brief run-in with the British press when they claimed she was putting her daughter in danger by trying to teach her to waterski without safety gear. Ever confident, Jackie simply laughed and brushed it off. She mothered her children as she wanted and took ill words from no one.

Jacqueline continued mothering her children as they grew into adulthood, as well. She was proud of their achievements, although she did not live to see them all. John F. Kennedy, Jr. passed the New York bar exam and eventually founded the political magazine *George*. Caroline Kennedy attended Harvard University and Columbia University. She worked for the Obama administration first as a campaign manager and then as the twenty-ninth United States Ambassador to Japan.

Upon discovering that her son was pursuing a pilot's license, she begged him to cease: "Please don't do it. There have been too many deaths in the family already."[ccv] For some reason, the Kennedy family had very bad luck with airplanes. The eldest of John F. Kennedy's uncles, Joe Kennedy, Jr., died when his plane exploded into pieces over the English Channel in the midst of World War II. Then, only a few years later, Kennedy's Aunt Kathleen Kennedy died when her plane crashed into France's Cévennes Mountains. Jackie's fears were obviously not unfounded.

Her worries did not simply end with their conversation about flying. Jacqueline had begun having a series of premonitions about her children, the strongest of which involved her son crashing and dying at the controls of his own plane. Even on her deathbed, she made her son swear that he would not pursue the life of a pilot; he did, indeed, die in a 1999 plane crash, but Jackie did not live to see it. Maybe the "Kennedy Curse" lived on. Maybe it is a myth. Either way, the Kennedy men had ill luck and died young.

Chapter Five: Campaign for Presidency

After four years of President Dwight Eisenhower's reign in the White House, many Americans felt it was time to move on to a Democrat administration in 1956. Among those looking for change, John F. Kennedy was included. Jacqueline fully supported her husband's intentions to try out his hand at higher politics. If nothing else, Kennedy would run for vice president alongside Adlai Stevenson. In the end, Kennedy did not win the vice-presidential slot, but he did get his name out there.[ccvi] Jackie's dislike for the media may have begun its obvious downward spiral at this point. Maxine Cheshire, a journalist, followed Jacqueline at the Democratic Convention, seeking a quote about her husband's endeavors, but she was having none of it. Onlookers say the very pregnant woman "hiked up her dress and broke into a run" to escape.[ccvii] This reaction was not very professional, but it made people laugh and somehow added to Jackie's charm.

Kennedy announced his candidacy for the presidency on January 3, 1960, thereby launching his campaign. In the beginning of the campaign, Jackie attended events with her husband, but her appearances grew less common when she discovered that she was pregnant. Due to her previous high-risk pregnancies, she decided to stay at home in Georgetown to watch after her health.[ccviii] She asked her husband numerous times to come home to spend a bit of time with her and their daughter, but JFK was reluctant to do so, arguing that he needed to focus entirely on his campaign.

The media gathered around their house, putting additional stress on Jacqueline during her pregnancy. Although she was not in the hot seat, she remained in the eye of the media. All of the couple's hard work paid off on July 13, 1960, and John F. Kennedy was nominated at the 1960 Democratic National Convention in Los Angeles as the proffered candidate for president of the United States. Due to her pregnancy, Jacqueline did not attend the event. She was growing more and more nervous about her pregnancy.

Kennedy flew home for a brief moment to have Thanksgiving with his family, but he had to fly back to Palm Beach that same night. When her due date was only three weeks away, she asked her husband to stay close: "Why can't you stay here until I have the baby and then we can go down together?"[ccix] JFK replied that he could not do so. Their friend Bill Walton said that three weeks "might as well have been six months to him. He was not about to put everything on hold just because Jackie was a little nervous. He had a country to run."[ccx] He left an upset wife behind him as he headed back to Palm Beach. His plane had barely lifted off the ground when Jacqueline was rushed to an emergency Caesarean section. As soon as he landed, he immediately turned around and rushed back to his wife and newborn son.

Although she was an exhausted mother, Jacqueline tried her best to maintain support of her husband's candidacy from home. In a weekly newspaper column called *Campaign Wife*, Jackie answered submitted questions and gave interviews.[ccxi] Additionally, her fashion choices drew a good bit of attention from the media. Before she gave birth, she wore maternity clothing that emphasized her pregnancy, rather than trying to hide it. This was a new idea for the American public, and they were a bit flabbergasted. The coin had two sides, though: she was admired for her personal style but criticized for her preference for expensive French clothing. She was named as one of the twelve best-dressed women in the world at one point.[ccxii] Jacqueline was not overly pleased with this attention; she often refused to discuss her wardrobe and instead drove the conversation toward the work she was doing for her husband's campaign.[ccxiii]

Chapter Six: First Lady

Jacqueline Kennedy Onassis at thirty-one years old became the third youngest first lady in American history. The Kennedy family presented the American public and the White House with a dramatic change from the Eisenhowers—they were young, affiliated with another political party, and involved with the media in different ways. Tina Sani Flaherty, in her book *What Jackie Taught Us: Lessons from the Remarkable Life of Jacqueline Kennedy Onassis*, says, "Together they symbolized a poignant time in our nation's history, when its innocence and optimism promised that anything was possible. They gave us hope and made us feel that each of us would be the best we could be."[ccxiv] Gil Troy, historian, says the Kennedy family "emphasized vague appearances rather than specific accomplishments or passionate commitments," relaying a "cool, TV-oriented culture."[ccxv] Jacqueline Kennedy did not feel very cool, though. She felt like she was being ogled at every moment of her life. Jacqueline said, "[It's] as though I have just turned into a piece of public property. It's really frightening to lose your anonymity at thirty-one."[ccxvi]

Just as Jackie was noted for her fashion experiences before her husband's presidency, she also gained a good bit of media fame after he was sworn into office. Jacqueline said at one point, "All the talk over what I wear and how I fix my hair has me amused, but it also puzzles me. What does my hairdo have to do with my husband's ability to be president?"[ccxvii] As the first lady, Jacqueline attempted to do what the United States public wanted and hired American designer

Oleg Cassini to design her wardrobe instead of continuing to buy more French couture.^{ccxviii} About Jacqueline, Cassini said, "The common misconception about her is that she wanted to become a fashion trendsetter. Nothing could be further from the truth. Jackie basically had her own carefully directed style. She dressed for herself. She wanted to be noticed, not copied. But it was clear from the beginning that anybody with Jackie's exotic beauty and high visibility was bound to have a profound influence on fashion."^{ccxix} Between 1961 and 1963, Jacqueline worked with Cassini on her most well-remembered ensembles. She actually spent $455,446 more on fashion than her husband's presidential salary of $100,000 in 1961.^{ccxx} These spending trends were not the beginning; rather, it was an old issue. Jackie's mother recalls having dinner at her daughter's house and marveling at her spending:

"We were having dinner there one night and Jack didn't get home until quite late, after we had finished dinner. He was having dinner on a tray. At that moment the room was entirely beige: the walls had been repainted a week or so before, and the furniture had all been upholstered in soft beige, and there was a vicuna rug over the sofa ... And let's see—rugs, curtains, upholstery, everything, was suddenly turned lovely different shades of beige. I knew how wildly expensive it is to paint things and upholster things and have curtains made, but I can remember Jack just saying to me, 'Mrs. Auchincloss, do you think we're prisoners of beige?'"^{ccxxi}

The pocketbook of Jacqueline knew no limits, and she was reluctant to live a life in which it needed to do so.

Jacqueline was also the first presidential wife to hire a press secretary. Her new hire, Pamela Turnure, helped her to manage media contact and to control how often and in which manner the presidential children and the Kennedys' daily activities were photographed.^{ccxxii} Although Turnure was President Kennedy's prior (and probably continuing) lover, she did her job well, capable of dealing with the press in a way that pleased Jacqueline. Jackie told Turnure, "You will be there as a buffer. My press relations will be minimum information given with maximum politeness ... I won't give any interviews, pose for photographs, etc. for the next four years. Pierre [Salinger, John F. Kennedy's press secretary] will bring in *Life* and *Look* or Stan [Tretick] a couple of times a year and we'll have an okay on it."[ccxxiii] Jacqueline thought that she could control what the media did while she was in the White House; she was mostly wrong.

In the media's eyes, Jackie was the perfect, ideal woman. Maurine Beasley, an academic scholar, claims that Jacqueline "created an unrealistic media expectation for first ladies that would challenge her successors."[ccxxiv] This media attention, although she did not want or appreciate it, allowed Jacqueline to gain positive attention on a global scale, gaining allies for the United States government and its Cold War policies.[ccxxv]

At this point in time, female reporters were often limited to providing information only on events and news involving the first lady. For this specific reason, Jacqueline was a godsend to the livelihood of female reporters, although she despised their attention. Everything she did was an opportunity for a news story. She traveled often, she hosted elaborate parties at the White House with big entertainment and extravagant decorating, she dressed in photo-worthy outfits daily, she ensured that her children and pets were presentable at all times, she rode horses and went boating, and she often visited the various Kennedy homes; all these occasions provided chances for good articles for all audiences. A reporter named Thomas said, "The irony is that Jackie Kennedy unwittingly gave a tremendous lift to me and many other women reporters in Washington by escalating our beat ... to instantaneous front-page news ... One biting quip form Jackie or a spill from a horse could launch a thousand headlines."[ccxxvi]

While Jacqueline made front-page news with her fashion statements, she is perhaps best known to many people for the time she dedicated to American history and art preservation. She hosted a multitude of events at the White House with the goal of bringing together elite politicians with artists to encourage mingling between the two groups. She wanted to found a Department of the Arts, a goal that remained unrealized, but she instead contributed to the establishment of the National Endowment for the Arts and the National Endowment for the Humanities, both of which are programs which continue to function and help the art programs and various artists to continue to prosper in the United States of America.

In all, Jacqueline's primary contribution to the Kennedy government was her project that aimed to restore and replenish the White House. Before her appointment as first lady, Jackie visited the White House twice—once as a tourist in 1941 and once as a guest of Mamie Eisenhower right before John F. Kennedy's inauguration.[ccxxvii] Her vision began growing during her second visit; she made a plan. Jacqueline wanted the White House to relay its historical importance, and she wondered why the furniture and décor did not display any significance whatsoever. Therefore, she made it her first major project as first lady to restore glory and historical character to the White House. She poured her entire self into the project. Lady Bird Johnson said that Jackie "was a worker, which I don't think was always quite recognized." Upon her visit to the White House after John F. Kennedy's election in 1960, Jacqueline was displeased to find that the state rooms resembled the lobby of a dreary Statler Hotel, which was no coincidence. In an attempt to save money, Harry Truman hired the New York department store B. Altman to provide furnishings for the mansion's main floor after the White House was gutted and reinforced with steel framing during a remodel in his presidency. Jackie was not pleased whatsoever with that choice of interior design.

Jacqueline met with interior decorator Sister Parish on her first day in the White House. Her plan was to make the family quarters more suitable for family living, as she felt there was an extreme lack in that department. Henceforth, she wanted a kitchen on the family floor and new rooms for her children. She was budgeted fifty thousand dollars for the project, and the money was soon gone. Letting nothing stand in the way of restoration, Jacqueline established a fine arts committee to direct the process as she spoke to Henry du Pont, an American furniture expert, for advice on some of the details.[ccxxviii] Soon, an excellent opportunity presented itself: the restoration teams would sell a White House guidebook to fund the White House restoration.[ccxxix] The guidebook became something of a relic. People bought it not because they needed it but rather because it would be helpful for a cause and it could later serve as memorabilia or an antique.

Jacqueline was a busy woman during her time in the White House. Not only did she work on the White House itself, but she also took part in redesigning and replanting the White House Rose Garden and East Garden with Rachel Lambert "Bunny" Mellon—American horticulturalist, gardener, philanthropist, and art collector. Along with these tasks, Jacqueline assisted in halting the destruction of historic homes in Lafayette Square in Washington, D.C. She felt they were an integral part of the capital's history and wanted them to continue holding role in the nation's history.[ccxxx] Therefore, she helped jumpstart a restoration project to take the place of the destruction.

The new first lady was particularly miffed when she discovered a long-standing tradition among former presidents. Before the Kennedys arrived in the White House, other presidential families formed a habit of taking furnishings and other items from the White House upon their departure, which led the historical structure to have a severe lack of historical items. Jacqueline took it upon herself to track down some of these thieved items, and she personally wrote to the previous White House families and other donors, asking that they return old pieces and provide new pieces if possible. Additionally, she initiated a Congressional bill that allowed the Smithsonian Institution to claim ownership of items in the White House so that future presidential families could not keep any of the furnishings when departing. In addition to these efforts, Jackie founded the White House Historical Association, the Committee for the Preservation of the White House, the position for a permanent Curator of the White

House, the White House Endowment Trust, and the White House Acquisition Trust.[ccxxxi]

Jacqueline's passion for the restoration project only grew during her time living in the White House. Reluctantly but hyperaware of the film's necessity, she took American television viewers on a virtual tour of the White House on 14 February 1962 as Charles Collingwood of CBS News followed alongside her. Jackie said, "I feel so strongly that the White House should have as fine a collection of American pictures as possible. It's so important—the setting in which the presidency is presented to the world, to foreign visitors. The American people should be proud of it. We have such a great civilization. So many foreigners don't realize it. I think that this house should be the place we see them best."[ccxxxii] Over fifty-six million people in the United States watched the virtual tour, and the video later made its way to 106 other countries, as well.[ccxxxiii] At the Emmy Awards in 1962, Jacqueline won a special Academy of Television Arts and Sciences Trustees Award, which Claudia Alta "Lady Bird" Johnson—Lyndon B. Johnson's wife—accepted on her behalf. Jackie was the only first lady to win an Emmy.[ccxxxiv]

During the same time period that she was redesigning the White House, Jackie was also working on the exterior of Air Force One, transforming the Oval Office into a space that resembled a living room, and altering the rituals for South Lawn arrival ceremonies and state dinners. All of her changes remain mostly intact after over fifty years. Jacqueline wrote once as a young woman that her goal was to become the "art director of the twentieth century." Many people claim that she achieved this dream through her role in the White House.

Although she spent a good amount of time in the White House, Jackie was up in the air and overseas for extended periods, too. Since she appeared popular among international dignitaries, the Kennedy administration took advantage of her position.[ccxxxv] For example, she impressed the French public with her ability to speak their language and her knowledge of French history.[ccxxxvi] After her trip, *Time* magazine noted jokingly, "There was also that fellow who came with her." Laughingly, President Kennedy said, "I am the man who accompanied Jacqueline Kennedy to Paris—and I have enjoyed it!"[ccxxxvii],[ccxxxviii] By herself or with her husband, she made more official visits to other countries than any of the preceding first ladies.[ccxxxix] Her name grew larger across the world, and her fame bloomed. In fact, when the Kennedys visited Vienna, Austria, Soviet premier Nikita Khrushchev said, "I'd like to shake her hand first," obviously referring to Jacqueline when asked to pose for a picture with President John F. Kennedy. Later, he sent her a puppy, the offspring of Strelka, which was the dog that had gone to space during a Soviet space mission.[ccxl]

Throughout her husband's presidency, Jackie continued to impress foreign dignitaries. The president of Pakistan, Ayub Khan, presented her with a horse named Sardar during her tour of India and Pakistan.[ccxli] Referring to the first lady's visits, Anne Chamberlin of *Life* magazine wrote that Jacqueline "conducted herself magnificently," but she did not draw the same massive crowds that Queen Elizabeth II and President Dwight Eisenhower had gathered on previous occasions.[ccxlii] Jackie let nothing slow her down, though. In addition to the previously named countries, she traveled to Afghanistan, Austria, Canada, Colombia, England, Greece, Italy, Mexico, Morocco, Turkey, and Venezuela.

Chapter Seven: Kennedy Assassination

If the general public knows nothing more about the life of Jacqueline, they have a shared, connected memory of the John F. Kennedy assassination and all the ill feelings that go along with the recollection. They remember the pink Chanel suit and the pillbox hat she wore when her husband was shot beside her. They remember the pictures, the newsreels, the articles. They remember the video of Jacqueline scrambling out of the back of the car, possibly reaching for pieces of her husband's skull.

John F. Kennedy and Jacqueline left the White House on November 21, 1963 for a trip to Texas. It was a relatively normal affair. The president was to speak at a lunch at the Trade Mart, and they had planned a 9.5-mile motorcade to take them there. In the back seat of the presidential limousine sat the Kennedys with Texas governor John Connally and his wife Nellie seated in front of them, while vice president Lyndon B. Johnson and his wife Lady Bird followed behind them in another car.[ccxliii]

Lady Bird Johnson said in her diary that "It all began so beautifully. After a drizzle in the morning, the sun came out bright and clear … The streets were lined with people—lots and lots of people—the children all smiling, placards, confetti, people waving from the windows." Everything was normal until a sharp sound rang over the crowd. Jackie recalled that she thought she heard a motorcycle backfiring after the motorcade turned onto Elm Street in Dealey Plaza. She did not realize the sound was a gunshot until governor John

Connally screamed. Lady Bird Johnson wrote: "There had been such a gala air about the day that I thought the noise must come from firecrackers—part of the celebration. Then the Secret Service men were down in the lead car. Over the car radio system, I heard, 'Let's get out of here!' and our Secret Service man, Rufus Youngblood, vaulted over the front seat on top of Lyndon, threw him to the floor, and said, 'Get down.'"[ccxliv] That one shot acted as a warning that the Kennedys did not register quite in time.

Within less that ten seconds, two more shots were fired, one of which hit John F. Kennedy in the head. In a panic, Jacqueline began climbing out of the back of the limousine. Secret Service agent Clint Hill ran toward her, urging her to move back into her seat. In this moment, Associated Press photographer Ike Atgens snapped one of the most iconic photos, which included Hill standing on the vehicle's back bumper. The photo was featured on the front page of newspapers across the world. The moment was a blur for everyone involved. Clint Hill later said that he thought Jacqueline was attempting to reach for a piece of her husband's skull.[ccxlv] Jackie later said that "[I saw pictures] of me climbing out the back. But I don't remember that at all."[ccxlvi]

Lady Bird Johnson wrote: "Senator Yarborough and I ducked our heads. The car accelerated terrifically—faster and faster. Then, suddenly, the brakes were put on so hard that I wondered if we were going to make it as we wheeled left and went around the corner. We pulled up to a building. I looked up and saw a sign, 'HOSPITAL.' Only then did I believe that this might be what it was. Senator Yarborough kept saying in an excited voice, 'Have they shot the President? Have they shot the President?' I said something like, 'No, it can't be.'"[ccxlvii] She recalls, "I cast one last look over my shoulder and saw in the President's car a bundle of pink, just like a drift of blossoms, lying in the back seat. It was Mrs. Kennedy lying over the President's body."[ccxlviii]

President John F. Kennedy was quickly taken to Dallas' Parkland Hospital. Jacqueline requested to be in the operating room, and she stood watching as the doctors operated on her husband diligently. Afterward, Jacqueline refused to remove her blood-stained clothing and said she regretted washing the blood off her face and hands. She told Lady Bird Johnson that she wanted "them to see what they have done to Jack."[ccxlix] In the face of such tragedy, Jacqueline was strong and angry.

Lady Bird Johnson recalls, "I looked at her. Mrs. Kennedy's dress was stained with blood. One leg was almost entirely covered with it and her right glove was caked, it was caked with blood—her husband's blood. Somehow that was the one of the most poignant sights—that immaculate woman exquisitely dressed, and caked in blood."[ccl] Jackie kept the pink Chanel dress on as Lyndon B. Johnson took the presidential oath on Air Force One. Robert Caro, Lyndon B. Johnson's biographer, said that Johnson wanted Jacqueline to be present in order to demonstrate to John F. Kennedy's supporters that he was a legitimate leader.[ccli] In 1964, the unwashed pink Chanel outfit was donated to the National Archives and Records Administration, but Caroline Kennedy, the Kennedys' daughter, asked that it not be displayed until 2103.

Jacqueline played a large part in planning her husband's state funeral. Modeled after Abraham Lincoln's service, the casket was closed, which Jacqueline wished, overruling her brother-in-law, Robert, who wanted an open casket.[cclii] They held the funeral service at the Cathedral of St. Matthew the Apostle in Washington, D.C., and buried President John F. Kennedy at Arlington National Cemetery. At the procession, Jackie led on foot and lit the eternal flame at the gravesite. "Jacqueline Kennedy has given the American people … one thing they have always lacked: Majesty," reported Lady Jeanne Campbell. For the first time in public, Jacqueline sobbed as Cardinal Cushing intoned the pontifical requiem.[ccliii] Clint Hill gave her his handkerchief and Lee Bouvier gave her a blue pill.[ccliv] She had both Arabella and

Patrick's caskets brought to be buried beside their father, and she would later be buried there, as well.

President Lyndon B. Johnson established the Warren Commission a week after the assassination. The Warren Commission's single goal was to investigate the murder, and Chief Justice Earl Warren led the efforts. After ten months, the Commission determined that Lee Harvey Oswald killed Kennedy alone with no partners.[cclv] Jacqueline was relatively disjoined from the efforts, saying that the investigation would not bring her husband back to life. After the burial, she stepped away from the public view. She appeared once at a ceremony in Washington that honored Secret Service agent Clint Hill who had climbed on top of the limousine to shield the Kennedys from the attacker.

Chapter Eight: Life Following the Assassination

The Dallas shooting followed Jacqueline for the rest of her life, but she slowly grew accustomed to the large switch in life trailing the tragedy. A week later, she said in an interview for *Life* magazine, "Don't let it be forgot, that once there was a spot, for one brief, shining moment that was known as Camelot. There'll be great presidents again … but there will never be another Camelot."[cclvi] The president often played Lerner and Loewe's music before bed, Jackie said, and she utilized Queen Guinevere's words from the musical to express her feelings of loss.[cclvii] For this reason, the Kennedy administration is referred to as the Camelot Era. Many historians and scholars say that Jacqueline thought of this idea and plotted a way for her family to be remembered. By connecting the Kennedy family to the legend of Arthur Pendragon, she made it seem as if her family ruled the United States as if they were aristocracy devoted to their kingdom. The thought has stuck around, so her idea must have held some wit and finesse.

A fortnight after the assassination, Jackie left the White House. She asked her Secret Service drivers to avoid routes that would take her within eyesight of the White House and visited only once again after leaving. In 1971, she and her children took an unphotographed, secretive trip to see Aaron Shikler's portraits of the Kennedy couple. At the time, the White House was under the rule of Richard Nixon, and she wrote him later to say, "A day I had always dreaded turned out to be one of the most precious ones I have spent with my children." She appreciated her time in the White House but found it necessary to remove herself from its presence.

On numerous occasions, the newly inaugurated president Lyndon B. Johnson attempted to "do something nice for Jackie." He knew how much she loved France and offered her an ambassadorship for the country, then for Mexico and Great Britain, as well, but she turned him down every time, wanting to remain removed. A week after her husband's death, she did request that the space center in Florida be renamed the John F. Kennedy Space Center, which the government humbly obliged. Later, Jacqueline said Johnson was kind and welcoming in her time of distress.[cclviii]

Jackie spent much of 1964 in mourning, making few appearances in public, although she did make a televised appearance on January 14, 1964 to thank everyone for the "hundreds of thousands of messages" they had sent to her since the tragedy befell her family. She attended a few memorial dedications to her husband over the following years and maintained a pivotal role in the establishment of the John F. Kennedy Presidential Library and Museum, which is near the University of Massachusetts in Boston.[cclix]

Even after her husband's death, Jacqueline served a large role in the American government, especially in foreign relations, whether she wanted it or not. In November 1967, during the Vietnam War, *Life* magazine called her "America's unofficial roving ambassador." Along with David Ormsby-Gore, the former British ambassador to the United States, she packed her bags and traveled to Cambodia to visit with Chief of State Norodom Sihanouk at the religious complex of Angkor Wat.[cclx] Historian Milton Osbourne called her visit "the start of the repair to Cambodia-US relations, which had been at a very low ebb."[cclxi] Additionally, in April 1968, she attended Martin Luther King, Jr.'s funeral services in Atlanta, Georgia, although she was nervous about the surrounding crowds and her likely flashbacks to her own husband's death.[cclxii]

After John F. Kennedy's assassination, Jacqueline closely bonded with her brother-in-law Robert F. Kennedy. She said he was "least like his father" out of all the Kennedy brothers. Early in her marriage, Robert Kennedy supported the couple when they had a miscarriage, and he stayed with her in the hospital.[cclxiii] Rumors say that something more happened between the two, just as many rumors say that she had an affair with Ted Kennedy, as well. Regardless of whatever may have happened, after Kennedy's death, his brother became a father figure to the Kennedy children and stayed close to them until he had to return to his own family and responsibilities as attorney general.[cclxiv]

Their relationship was a familiar one if not an intimate one, and Robert Kennedy credits Jackie for encouraging him to remain in politics and supporting his 1964 run for the United States Senate as a representative of New York.[cclxv] After 1968, when President Lyndon B. Johnson lost popularity during the Tet offensive, Robert Kennedy's advisors encouraged him to enter the upcoming presidential race. Many people were curious about this turn of events, wondering if he would follow in his brother's footsteps within politics. When asked about his intentions, Kennedy said, "That depends on what Jackie wants me to do."[cclxvi] He did not want to pursue the presidency if it was going to offend her. Jacqueline still held a pit of worry in her stomach and was concerned that Robert Kennedy would fall into the same ending as her husband. She said that there was "so much hatred" in the United States. Although she was worried, Jackie campaigned for her brother-in-law and gave him all her support in his endeavor. A few times, she even said that she hoped the Kennedy family would be able to serve the White House again.[cclxvii] Those moments were her most hopeful throughout the campaign.

For a while, the Kennedy train was trekking along smoothly, but on June 5, 1968, just after midnight, Robert Kennedy faced the same trauma as his brother. He was shot and mortally wounded soon after he and his supporters celebrated his victory in the California Democratic presidential primary.[cclxviii] He was rushed to a hospital where Jacqueline and his other family members joined, but he did not regain consciousness and died only twenty-six hours after the shooting.[cclxix] And thus, another Kennedy fell to the "Kennedy Curse."

After her brother-in-law's death, Jackie fell into yet another deep depression, similar to the one she experienced after her husband's assassination. She was drenched in fear: "If they're killing Kennedys, then my children are targets ... I want to get out of this country."[cclxx] For a while, she achieved that goal. She married her friend (and possibly her prior lover) Aristotle Onassis on October 20, 1968. He was a wealthy Greek man who could provide security and privacy for her family. According to Hunt and Batcher, "For the most recognizable woman in the world, a man who owned an airline and a private Greek island was a sensible choice. Their marriage gave her the freedom to travel, live, and spend as she desired."[cclxxi]

The wedding was on Onassis' private island, Skorpios, in the Ionian Sea. With this marriage, Jacqueline lost her right to Secret Service protection, which is given only to widows of United States presidents. This fact made her nervous, but she felt that her trade-out would also ensure security. Leaving her past behind her, she officially changed her name to Jacqueline Onassis. Her marriage brought a good bit of ill publicity around her family. Aristotle Onassis was divorced, but his ex-wife was still living, and the public speculated that Jacqueline may be excommunicated by the Roman Catholic Church for her sin of marrying a divorced man. Some of the Kennedys even pushed for that result, thinking that she had betrayed their family.

During this time, the paparazzi began following her everywhere again, waiting for a scandalous story. They nicknamed her "Jackie O."[cclxxii] The marriage soured after a couple of years, and they began to live separately for much of the time. When Aristotle Onassis' son Alexander died in a plane crash in 1973, his health began deteriorating quickly, and he died in Paris at age sixty-nine of respiratory failure on March 15, 1975. It seemed as if Jacqueline did not have much luck when it came to male lovers and friends.

Chapter Nine: Coming to an End

When her second husband died, Jacqueline returned to the United States and lived on and off in Martha's Vineyard, Manhattan, and the Kennedy Compound in Hyannis, Massachusetts. Though she suffered long stints of severe depression, she attempted to keep herself busy with work, her children, and the rest of the Kennedy family.

Although Jackie presented herself as a woman who did not quite lean toward feminism during her husband's presidency, her opinions changed over time. She did not remain the iconic woman of the pre-feminist era in the early 1960s. In her oral history, Jacqueline said that women should avoid politics because they are "too emotional" and should instead be subordinate to their husbands in the "best" marriages. After the death of her second husband, she altered that mindset and geared toward becoming a career woman.

She began working as a New York editor at Viking, followed by another editorial job she took at Doubleday. In her line of work, she published art books, memoirs, and histories, among other things. She steadily grew a reputation as a genuine colleague who was not afraid to do the dirty work in line editing. In this space, she grew as a person during the time when many American women were redefining their roles in the workplace and the home. She said, "What has been sad for many women of my generation is that they weren't supposed to work if they had families ... What were they going to do when their children were grown—watch the raindrops coming down the windowpane?" She believed in keeping busy, in entertaining the mind and the heart with goals and deadlines. Jacqueline addresses the problematic societal standards at their core, a call for American women to take control of their own lives.

For two years, she held a consulting editorial position at Viking Press. She resigned in 1977 when *The New York Times* falsely accused her of collaborating with Viking to produce the Jeffrey Archer novel *Should We Tell the President?*, a fictional novel which described a time in which Ted Kennedy was elected as president and laid out an assassination plot against him.[cclxxiii] Jacqueline was horrified with the thought and considered it best to distance herself. At Doubleday, Jackie worked for John Turner Sargent, Sr., as an associate editor. She edited quite a few books for the company, including titles such as Larry Gonick's *The Cartoon History of the Universe*, all three volumes of the English version of Naghib Mahfuz's *Cairo Trilogy*, and autobiographies for ballerina Gelsey Kirkland, singer-songwriter Carly Simon, and the fashionista Diana Vreeland. She also encouraged Dorothy West, the last surviving member of the Harlem Renaissance and her neighbor at Martha's Vineyard, to complete *The Wedding*, a novel that outlined a multi-generational story about wealth, power, race, and class in the United States.

Jacqueline kept herself busy in other ways, as well. Continuing her passion for preservation and American history, she took part in many cultural and architectural preservation projects. Perhaps most notably, she oversaw a historic preservation campaign to save and renovate New York's Grand Central Terminal. She loved New York City and held its culture close to her heart. She fought hard to preserve part of its history. The terminal holds a plaque that acknowledges her role in the endeavor. Furthermore, she played a large part in protesting the building of a skyscraper that would have engulfed Central Park in shadow. The building project was cancelled, although another took its place in 2003.

The press never quite lost its obsession with Jacqueline. Ron Galella was notorious for following her around, taking pictures of her everyday activities and being a general pest, in her opinion. Without her permission, he snapped countless photographs. Eventually, she had to obtain a restraining order against him, which brought the issues of paparazzi photography to the forefront of concerning problems in the United States of America. Americans were asking questions. Should paparazzi be allowed to infiltrate others' lives? Do the American people need to know the private facts about their politicians' lives? Who is to make that decision?

She avoided political events for almost an entire decade but attended the 1976 Democratic National Convention. Here, she surprised everyone as she appeared in the visitors' gallery.[cclxxiv] Along with her mother-in-law Rose Kennedy, Jackie appeared at Faneuil Hall in Boston two years later. Here, Ted Kennedy announced that he would be challenging incumbent President Jimmy Carter for the Democratic nomination for president.[cclxxv] Jackie participated in the campaign, supporting Ted Kennedy, but the endeavor was unsuccessful.[cclxxvi]

This instance was not the end of her play with politics. Jacqueline supported Bill Clinton in the early 1990s and contributed funds to his presidential campaign. She met with Hillary Rodham Clinton, Bill Clinton's wife, after he won the presidency and chatted with her about rearing children in the cutthroat environment that was the White House. Under Bill Clinton's presidency, Hillary Clinton invited Jacqueline to visit the White House, but she declined, saying she appreciated the gesture but would rather not be in that space. After Jackie's death, her son John wrote Hillary Clinton to say, "Since she left Washington, I believe she resisted ever connecting with it emotionally—or the institutional demands of being a former First Lady. It had much to do with the memories stirred and her desires to resist being cast in a lifelong role that didn't quite fit." In her memoir *Living History,* Hillary Clinton wrote that Jacqueline was "a source of inspiration and advice for me."[cclxxvii] Democratic consultant Ann Lewis said that Jacqueline interacted and supported the Clinton family "in a way she has not always acted toward leading Democrats in the past."[cclxxviii]

Later in the same year, Jackie began to experience health issues. During a fox hunt in Middleburg, Virginia, in 1993, her horse threw her off its back, and her comrades rushed her to the hospital, afraid that she was hurt badly.[cclxxix] The doctor found a swollen lymph node in her groin, which he thought was an infection, but Jacqueline developed new symptoms, including a stomach ache and swollen lymph nodes in her neck, within the next month. Upon a new visit to the doctor, she was diagnosed with anaplastic large-cell lymphoma.[cclxxx] In January 1994, Jacqueline began chemotherapy and announced the diagnosis publicly. Although she was undergoing a plethora of treatments, the cancer spread to her spinal cord and brain by March and to her liver by May. Accepting that it was time for her to go, she left New York Hospital—Cornell Medical Center on May 18, 1994 and died the next night in her home at 10:15. Jacqueline was only sixty-four years old at the time of her death.[cclxxxi]

Jackie's death hit the nation pretty hard, especially the Democrats who still believed in her husband's policies. She was remembered in the fashion community, the architectural community, historical societies, political circles, academic institutions, and more. Needless to say, her name will not soon be forgotten.

When speaking to the media after his mother's demise, John F. Kennedy, Jr. said, "My mother died surrounded by her friends and her family and her books, and the people and the things that she loved. She did it in her very own way, and on her own terms, and we all feel lucky for that."[cclxxxii] The funeral was held near Jackie's home at the Church of St. Ignatius Loyola at the same parish where she was baptized in 1929 and reached confirmation as a teenager. Her life came full circle. Jacqueline was buried at Arlington National Cemetery in Arlington, Virginia, next to her husband, President John F. Kennedy, and their two children, Patrick and their stillborn daughter Arabella. At her service, President Bill Clinton gave the eulogy, a great honor for her family.

At the time of her death, Jacqueline was survived by her children Caroline and John, Jr., three grandchildren, her sister Lee Radziwill, her son-in-law Edwin Schlossberg, and her half-brother James Lee Auchincloss. She was able to take comfort in the fact that her children had avoided the infamous "Kennedy Curse."[cclxxxiii]

Chapter Ten: Ongoing Iconic Figure

Jackie became a global fashion icon during her husband's presidency, but she was well known for a long while afterward. Since she preferred French couture but needed to conform to American design, she wrote to fashion editor Diana Vreeland and asked for American designers who could replicate the Paris look with "terribly simply, covered-up clothes." Vreeland thought on it for a while and recommended Norman Norell, who produced simplistic and high-quality work; Norell was known as America's First Designer. Additionally, she mentioned Ben Zuckerman, an American designer who often reproduced Paris couture, and Stella Sloat, another American designer who sometimes produced Givenchy look-alikes.[cclxxxiv] Jacqueline was thankful for the recommendations, as she wanted to keep her personal style that she adopted from Paris but also wanted to conform to the first lady that the American people wanted.

In her position as first lady, Jackie wore simple, clean-cut suits with modest skirts that fell to the middle of her knees, sleeveless A-line dresses, three-quarter sleeves on notch-collar jackets, gloves that rose above her elbows, pillbox hats, and low pumps.[cclxxxv] If nothing else is to be said, Jacqueline was quite proper and covered in her clothing most of the time. One would never guess upon first glance that her family could hold any scandalous secrets. Kenneth Battelle, or Mr. Kenneth as he is more commonly known, was famous for his work with women's hair; he created Jacqueline's bouffant hairstyle and worked for the first lady from 1954 to 1986.[cclxxxvi] The hairstyle he created for the first lady was often scathingly referred to as a "grown-up exaggeration of little girls' hair" with the amount of poof it contained.

After her years in the White House, Jackie's fashion altered a bit. She began wearing large lapel jackets, gypsy skirts, wide-leg pantsuits, silk head scarves and rounded dark sunglasses. People were a little shocked when she started wearing jeans in public. One of her signature looks consisted of white jeans with no belt, accompanied by a black turtleneck that she chose to pull down over her hips instead of tucking in her pants. Somehow, although covering, these clothes showed more of Jackie's body. They were not the clothing of the aristocracy. Rather, she wore common clothing that looked glitzier than normal. She looked more like a high-fashioned, average woman than the president's wife.

Jacqueline was also well known for her jewelry collection. Designed by American jeweler Kenneth Jay Lane, a triple-strand pearl necklace was her signature piece of jewelry when she served as first lady in the White House. Another piece she often wore was a strawberry brooch—often called the "berry brooch"—that was composed of two clustered strawberries made of rubies with stems and leaves of diamonds; this piece was designed by a French jeweler by the name of Jean Schlumberger for Tiffany & Co. President John F. Kennedy presented it to his wife a few days before his inauguration in January 1961 as a gift for their new life. Jackie held other pieces by Schlumberger, as well. In fact, she wore his gold and enamel bracelets so often that the press called them "Jackie bracelets" in the early and mid-1960s. Additionally, she wore his gold and white enamel "banana" earrings often. Although she appreciated the jewelry aforementioned, she was perhaps most fond of jewelry designed by Van Cleef & Arpels, which she wore throughout three decades—the 1950s, 1960s, and 1970s. Almost every day, she wore the Van Cleef & Arpels wedding ring President Kennedy gave her. It was her most sentimental piece of jewelry, and she was reluctant to leave it out of her sight for long.

In 1965, Jacqueline was granted entry to the International Best Dressed List Hall of Fame.[cclxxxvii] Even now, quite a few of her outfits are held and preserved at the John F. Kennedy Library and Museum, and the Metropolitan Museum of Art in New York exhibited pieces from the collection in 2001; the exhibition focused on her time as first lady and was called "Jacqueline Kennedy: The White House Years."[cclxxxviii] Most of the pieces are representative of her most important days in the White House, pieces she wore to important events and meetings both in the United States and overseas.

Jacqueline' name lived on long after she died and seems still to hold a high meaning. In 1995, a high school in New York City was dubbed Jacqueline Kennedy Onassis High School for International Careers. In Central Park, the main reservoir was renamed as the Jacqueline Kennedy Onassis Reservoir in her honor.[cclxxxix] The Municipal Art Society of New York has a Jacqueline Kennedy Onassis Medal that they present to individuals whose influence, work, and deeds have contributed outstandingly to the city of New York. The medal was named thus due to Jackie's preservation efforts in regard to New York City's architecture. At George Washington University, Jacqueline has a residence hall named after her. Additionally, the Kennedy couple's names were included on the list of people aboard the Japanese Kaguya mission as part of The Planetary Society's "Wish Upon the Moon" campaign, while their names were also listed aboard NASA's Lunar Reconnaissance Orbiter mission.[ccxc] These instances are simply a few of the honors that have been given to Jacqueline both prior and post her death.

Jacqueline was a powerful woman who will not be forgotten easily. She stood her ground in both the public and private spectrum, advising her husband secretly and providing a role model for the public. Not only did she serve as first lady, but she also worked long and hard hours as a mother within the White House and raised her children as a single parent after the death of her husband. She put so much of her effort into restoring parts of the United States' history from creating a lasting legacy at the White House with her renovating of everything within its four walls to her work with the New York Grand Central Station as she fought to keep it alive and running to the best of its ability. She was a busy woman. Over her life, she grew as a person, taking new ideas in her stride and becoming a strong, independent idol for other women in the United States and across the world. Much can be said about the scandalous acts that happened within the four walls of the White House, but we can all be sure of one thing: the legacy of Jackie Kennedy will live on forever.

Help requested

If you enjoyed this particular part on Jackie Kennedy, then it would be really appreciated it if you would post a short review for the book on Amazon.

Thanks for your support!

Preview of World War 2
A Captivating Guide from Beginning to End

Introduction

The Second World War was one of the most traumatic events in human history. Across the world, existing conflicts became connected, entangling nations in a vast web of violence. It was fought on land, sea, and air, touching every inhabited continent. Over 55 million people died, some of them combatants, some civilians caught up in the violence, and some murdered by their own governments.

It was the war that unleashed the Holocaust and the atomic bomb upon the world. But it was also a war that featured acts of courage and self-sacrifice on every side.

The world would never be the same again.

Chapter 1 – The Rising Tide

The Second World War grew out of conflicts in two parts of the world: Europe and East Asia. Though the two would eventually become entangled, it's easier to understand the causes of the war by looking at them separately.

Europe's problems were rooted in centuries of competition between powerful nations crammed together on a small and densely populated continent. Most of the world's toughest, most stubborn, and most ambitious kids were crammed together in a single small playground. Conflict was all but inevitable.

The most recent large European conflict had been the First World War. This was the first industrialized war, a hugely traumatic event for all the participants. In the aftermath, Germany was severely punished for its aggression by the victorious Allied powers. The remains of the Austro-Hungarian empire fell apart, creating instability in the east. And the Russian Empire, whose government had been overthrown during the turmoil of the war, became the Union of Soviet Socialist Republics (USSR), the first global power to adopt the new ideology of communism.

From this situation of instability, a new form of politics emerged. Across Europe, extreme right-wing parties adopted ultra-nationalistic views. Many of them incorporated ideas of racial superiority. Most were strongly influenced by the fear of communism. All relied on scapegoating outsiders to make themselves more powerful.

The first to reach prominence was the Fascist Party in Italy under Benito Mussolini. Mussolini was a veteran soldier, gifted orator, and skilled administrator. He rallied disenchanted left-wingers and those who felt put down by corrupt politicians and forceful trade unions. Using a mixture of persuasion and intimidation, he won the 1922 election and became prime minister. Through a series of laws, he turned his country into a one-party dictatorship. Most of his achievements were domestic, bringing order and efficiency at the price of freedom, but he also had ambitions abroad. He wanted Italy to be a colonial power like Britain or France, and so in 1935-6 his forces conquered Abyssinia.

Mussolini was surpassed in almost every way by the man who reached power in Germany a decade later—Adolph Hitler. A decorated veteran of the First World War, Hitler was embittered at the Versailles Treaty, which imposed crushing restrictions upon Germany in the aftermath of the war. He developed a monstrous ideology that combined racism, homophobia, and a bitter hatred of communism. Like Mussolini, he brought together oratory and street violence to seize control of Germany. Once elected chancellor in 1933, he purged all opposition and had himself made Führer, the nation's "leader" or "guide." He then escalated the rearmament of Germany, casting off the shackles of Versailles.

Hitler and Mussolini intervened in the Spanish Civil War of 1936-9. Rather than have their nations join the war, they sent parts of their armed forces to support Franco's right-wing armies, testing new military technology and tactics while ensuring the victory of a man they expected to be an ally—a man who would in fact keep his nation out of the coming war for Europe.

Meanwhile, Hitler was playing a game of chicken with the other European powers. In March 1936, he occupied the Rhineland, a part of Germany that had been demilitarized after the war. Two years later, he annexed his own homeland of Austria, with its large German-speaking population. He occupied parts of Czechoslovakia that fall and finished the job off the following spring. At every turn, the rest of Europe backed down rather than go to war to protect less powerful nations.

Meanwhile, in Asia, the Chinese revolutions of 1911 and 1913, along with the Chinese Civil War that broke out in 1927, had triggered a parallel period of instability. Nationalists and communists battled for control of a vast nation, destroying the regional balance of power.

Japan was a nation on the rise. Economic growth had created a sense of ambition which had then been threatened by a downturn in the 1930s. Interventions by Western powers, including their colonies in Asia and a restrictive naval treaty of 1930, embittered many in Japan, who saw the Europeans and Americans as colonialist outsiders meddling in their part of the world.

The Japanese began a period of expansion, looking to increase their political dominance and their control of valuable raw resources. They invaded Chinese Manchuria in 1931 and from then on kept encroaching on Chinese territory. At last, in 1937, the Chinese nationalist leader Chiang Kai-Shek gave up on his previous policy of giving ground to buy himself time. A minor skirmish escalated into the Second Sino-Japanese War.

From an Asian point of view, the war had already begun. But it would be Hitler who pushed Europe over the brink and gave the war its Western start date of 1939.

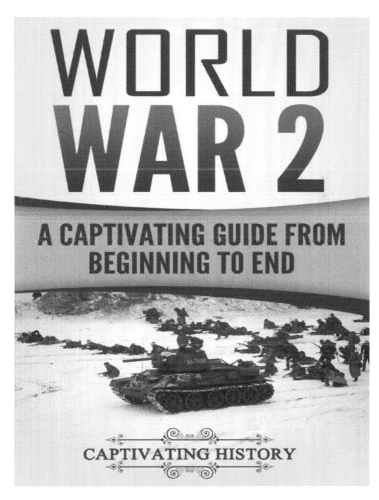

Check out this book!

Preview of Winston Churchill:
A Captivating Guide to the Life of Winston S. Churchill

Introduction

As a British politician who was well known for serving twice as prime minister for the United Kingdom and as an infamous war organizer, leader Winston S. Churchill filled his long life with achievements and recognition plotted throughout every modern history book. Most famously, he led Great Britain into victory over Nazi Germany during World War II in his first run as prime minister and played an essential role in negotiating peace once the war reached an unsteady end. Commonly, his name is associated as one of the "Big Three" alongside United States President Franklin D. Roosevelt and Soviet Union leader Joseph Stalin. In unity, the three men helped lead the world to a resolution from the violence and terror that reigned in World War II.

Winston Churchill was more than a military and government leader, though. He lived an entire life full of accomplishments that defined him as a singular person, rather than a government and military leader. In 1953, he won the Nobel Prize for Literature for his "mastery of historical and biographical description as well as for brilliant oratory in defending exalted human values."[ccxci] Although he maintained a somewhat monotone voice over the radio, Churchill excelled in speaking to live crowds as he imparted encouraging words and recounted tales of his life adventures. On top of these accomplishments as a writer and a trailblazer, Churchill is famous for his endless reserves of energy and his need for little sleep, which allowed him to pursue many projects and hobbies outside of his governmental duties.[ccxcii] Among many other possible descriptions,

Winton Churchill categorizes as a father, a husband, a painter, a war hero, a politician, a soldier, a smoker, a gambler, and a philosopher.

Any general biography of Winston Churchill will provide an overview of his greatest achievements, but Churchill had other goals and desires that are often ignored and forgotten. What were they? Churchill had a family—a childhood and children of his own—and a political career that began at a young age. He spoke with and entertained some of the biggest names in the world, within both the political and social realms. How did he interact with Franklin D. Roosevelt? With Mahatma Gandhi? Beneath the accolades and accomplishments lies one important question: Who was Winston Churchill out of the spotlight? What were his struggles and personal goals? Was he an average man in some ways? The following book is an outline of Churchill's life that not only gives a brief overview of his best-known feats but also provides a glimpse into who he was as a person.

Chapter One: Churchill's Personal Life

Often, people feel they know much about Winston Churchill as a servant to his country from easily attained and general information, but they know little about Churchill's personal life. Churchill was a husband, a father, a painter, and a historian, among many other things. While he also maintains the status of a war hero and prime minister, he was much more in life. His aspirations and desires were a large part of who he was and how he attained his goals.

An important part of every story lies within the family unit. In 1904, Winston attended a ball in Crewe House—the home of the Earl of Crewe and his wife, Margaret Primrose—where he met Clementine Hozier, the granddaughter of the 10th Earl of Airlie.[ccxciii] In 1908, they found themselves drawn together at another event, hosted by Lady St. Helier. Imaginably, they were instantly compatible because Churchill proposed to Clementine Hozier at Blenheim Palace, his childhood home, later that year, and they married shortly after.[ccxciv]

Over the course of their marriage, Winston and Clementine Churchill had five children: Diana, Randolph, Sarah, Marigold Frances, and Mary. Unfortunately, Marigold grew fatally ill just short of three years after she was born, and the family buried her in the Kensal Green Cemetery.[ccxcv] Their other children did not suffer the same fate but provided very interesting personalities and habits which the Churchills had to accommodate on very individual levels. Diana was rather flippant and brought her parents great duress. After two failed marriages and three children, Diana committed suicide in 1963. Randolph, after failing to enter parliament several times, finally found acceptance as a Conservative member of parliament for Preston between 1940 and 1945 and continued to become a successful journalist who began Winston S. Churchill's official biography in the 1960s.[ccxcvi] Like his sister, Randolph had two unsuccessful marriages. Additionally, he had two children. Sarah took a career in dramatics, which worked well for a while, but she had the same luck with her love life as her siblings in that she entered two marriages, which ultimately failed, and was then widowed after a third marriage. Mary was the only child who caused her parents little worry or grief. She provided heavy support for them both, especially her mother. Mary's husband, Christopher Soames, was an Assistant Military Attaché in Paris who later found success in parliament. They had five children, and Nicholas, the eldest, was a prominent member of the Conservative Party in his own time.

Although they spent long periods of time apart from one another, Winston and Clementine Churchill maintained a successful marriage, or, rather, as successful as most long marriages prove, generally. As all couples, they had their faults, fights, and failings. In one instance, Clementine hurled a dish of spinach at Churchill, which reportedly missed and splattered behind him. Additionally, she never quite forgave Churchill for buying Chartwell without expressly involving her in the purchase decision, and she brought up her resentment from time to time with a bitter grudge. As stated by Churchill College at Cambridge, "Clementine was high principled and high strung; Winston was stubborn and ambitious," a volatile combination of personality traits within a married couple.[ccxcvii]

Churchill spent a good portion of time away from his family, both on business and on holiday. It was a well-known fact that Winston Churchill put work first, but he was devoted to his children, regardless, although he enjoyed spending time abroad with friends and acquaintances much more than his wife and left his children at home; Clementine Churchill often "found the company tedious" and refused to accompany him.[ccxcviii] Occasionally, the family would take holidays together, but more often than not, they began taking vacations apart. Churchill holidayed with regularity, visiting wealthy friends in the Mediterranean and cruising with Aristotle Onassis, Greek millionaire ship-owner.[ccxcix] In all, they took eight cruises together. Once when they passed through the Dardanelles, Onassis instructed his crew to pass quietly and during the night so as to avoid drudging up Churchill's bad members of the location.

Winston Churchill's close friends included Professor Lindemann, along with Birkenhead, Beaverbrook, and Bracke—cheerfully dubbed "the three Bs"—of whom Clementine Churchill was never particularly fond. Although Clementine did not often travel with Churchill, the two entertained often as a couple, and their guests included the likes of Charlie Chaplin, Albert Einstein, and Lawrence of Arabia.

In addition to entertaining both his friends and family members, Winston Churchill engaged quite a few personal hobbies. As an amateur artist, Churchill enjoyed painting and employed a special gusto after resigning in 1915 as First Lord of the Admiralty.[ccc] Paul Maze, a friend of Churchill's whom he met in World War I, taught him to paint early during Churchill's career while providing both companionship and influence. Throughout his painting career, Churchill's skills grew stronger. Churchill is particularly known for his impressionist landscape paintings, and he composed many of these works of art while on holiday in Egypt, Morocco, or the South of France. Not wanting to paint under his own title, Churchill utilized the name "Charles Morin" as a pseudonym and reached the point where he rarely left his home without his painting supplies. Any time he traveled, he tried to slip away for a few moments so that he could spend time with his paints and canvas. Even when Churchill was touring France's Maginot Line in 1939, he still managed to paint with his friends near Dreux.[ccci]

Painting was only one of many hobbies Winston employed to pass his free time. Maybe unexpectedly, one of Churchill's greatest vices was a slight gambling addiction, and he lost a small fortune when the American stock market crashed in 1929. Although he maintained a famous name and arose from an upper-class family, Churchill did not believe his income supported his established lifestyle, and the 1929 crash didn't help cushion his ever-slimming pockets. Churchill's income while out of office arrived primarily from book sales and opinion pieces; therefore, he wrote often and well. Winston Churchill has a small library under his name, which includes a novel, two biographies, three volumes of memoirs, and several historical works. In 1953, he gained the Nobel Prize for Literature, and two of his most famous works brought international fame: The Second World War, his six-volume memoir, and *A History of the English-Speaking Peoples*, a four-volume history covering the period from Caesar's invasions of Britain to the beginning of World War I. Additionally, many of Churchill's speeches are in print, such as *Into Battle,* published in the United States under *Blood, Sweat, and Tears,* which *Life Magazine* included as one of the 100 most astounding books published between 1924 and 1944.[cccii]

In his spare time at home, Churchill also constructed buildings and garden walls at his house in Chartwell. A few major works he undertook at the country home were building a dam, a swimming pool, and a red brick wall to surround the vegetable garden, as well as retiling a cottage at the end of his garden. In addition to these home improvements, Churchill bought an adjoining farm in 1946 and took up farming.[ccciii] On the side, he also bred butterflies, an interest left over from his time in India.[ccciv] Moreover, Churchill found great interest in science and technology, delving into a stint of writing popular-science essays on evolution and fusion power. In *Are We Alone in the Universe?*, a mostly forgotten piece of writing, Churchill investigated in an unpublished manuscript the possibility of extraterrestrial life.

To top it all off, Churchill began dabbling in horse-racing in 1949 and took advice from his son-in-law, Christopher Soames, on his first purchase, a three-year-old gray colt named Colonist II, the first of many thoroughbreds. In 1950, Churchill was initiated into the Jockey Club, which much pleased him.[cccv]

All in all, Winston S. Churchill had a personal life full of odds-and-ends hobbies, similar to that of any common person. Historians pay close attention to his feats and follies, hoping to gain more insight into the mind of Winston Churchill, the fascinating man who left his mark on history in a way unlike any other. Churchill was a normal man, too, though. He cared for his family, enjoyed the small things in life, and felt that his efforts could be used in many ways.

Chapter Two: Winston S. Churchill's Mental Health

Scholars have long debated the topic of Winston Churchill's mental health, and a wide variety of opinions scatter in several places in accordance to the public figure's mindfulness. Some claim that he had clinical depression while others argue that he suffered from bipolar disorder. Still others suggest that he suffered from no mental disparity; instead, this group of scholars believe he was a powerful man who sometimes needed personal space and tended to think reflectively.

With the 1966 appearance of Lord Moran's memoirs, which describe his years as Churchill's doctor, came a greater understanding of Winston Churchill's mind. Moran claims that Churchill casually utilized the nickname "Black Dog" for his long fits of strenuous depression.[cccvi] From this small bit of information, many scholars find it safe to speculate that Churchill suffered from clinical depression at various points in his life.

Anthony Storrs—English psychiatrist, psychoanalyst, and author—analyzed and developed theories on Churchill's mental state based upon Moran's writings. Unfortunately, Moran did not keep updated or accurate notes on Churchill. Rather, he primarily based his writings on his own memory and on secondhand sources. A poor note-taker, Moran arbitrarily dated entries and wrote down claims from people other than Churchill. For example, one of the "Black Dog" entries, labeled as August 14, 1944, was based on a conversation with

Brendan Bracken who said in 1958 that Churchill seemed to be falling into "the inborn melancholia of the Churchill blood" at the end of World War II.

Although Churchill did not receive medication for his presumed depression, Moran notes that he prescribed amphetamines for big speeches after the autumn of 1953 to battle against the lasting effects of Churchill's stroke. During his lifetime, Churchill himself wrote about "Black Dog" only once. In a letter to his wife in 1911, he writes that a relative found successful treatment for depression at the hands of a German doctor. In his book *Painting as a Pastime,* Churchill notes that he suffers from "worry and mental overstrain [experienced] by persons who, over prolonged period, have to bear exceptional responsibilities and discharge duties upon a very large scale."[cccvii]

If the words of Lord Moran are to be believed, Winston often found joy in whiskey, soda, and his cigar. His book illustrates that Churchill fell into foul moods after military defeats, but these reactions are surely normal for any human who experiences a range of feelings. As many people with and without depression often do, it seems as if Churchill found methods of distraction, such as his many hobbies that led him to labor outside, paint, and travel.

During the war, Churchill grew feebler in regard to his physical health as well. In December 1941, he had a heart attack while at the White House and again in December 1942 when he had pneumonia. Disregarding the state of his body, he traveled over 100,000 miles under the pseudonym Colonel Warden during the war to meet with the Allies and other leaders.[cccviii] Some scholars speculate that Winston S. Churchill's mental illness could partially derive from physical illness, but that theory is mere speculation as with all the other evidence.

Carol Brekenridge, who worked for twenty years in outpatient mental health, presents a few different opinions on Churchill's depression. She suggests that Churchill exhibited no particular signs of severe depression or bipolar disorder. She proposes instead that he had attention deficit disorder with hyperactivity (ADD-H). According to Brekenridge, "Bipolar Disorder is a severely disabling mental illness. Without medication victims have difficulty maintaining relationships or employment. Their lives are chaotic, and often unproductive. They are unable to focus and lack the energy to martial their thoughts even to write a convincing letter to the editor, much less fifty books. They are not likely to create 500 paintings or support a family of five in an upper-class way of life, or become one of the world's most highly paid journalists."[cccix]

The Diagnostic and Statistical Manual of Mental Disorders (DSM) created nine criteria for "Major Depressive Episodes," which the DSM notates cannot be due to a medical condition: depressed mood, diminished interest or pleasure, significant weight change, insomnia or hypersomnia, psychomotor agitation or retardation, fatigue or loss of energy, feelings of worthlessness/inappropriate guilt, diminished concentration/indecisiveness, and recurrent thoughts of death. Winston Churchill maintained very few traits that fit into any of these categories. Rather, he was an overachiever who lived within a high-stress environment for most of his life. Therefore, he experienced some high-stress situations that led to anxiety, but he handled them well for the most part. Almost acting as an opposition to the outlined categories for depression, Churchill was active, curious, and excited for hobbies and side-projects.

From current information, it is near impossible to determine a diagnosis for Churchill's mental health. What historians and psychiatrists do know, however, is that Churchill never let his "Black Dog" keep him from achieving or pursuing anything in life.

Continue reading!

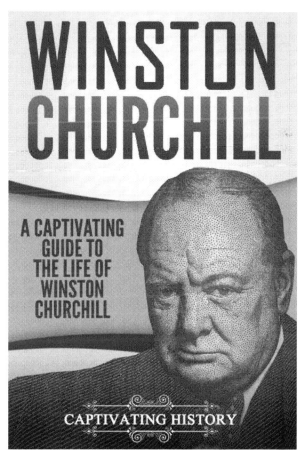

Check out this book!

Preview of Franklin Roosevelt: *A Captivating Guide to the Life of FDR*

Introduction

As the thirty-second president of the United States of America, Franklin Delano Roosevelt (30 January 1882—12 April 1945) is a common household name in both his home country and the world. Known as the man who led the United States through the Great Depression and World War II, Roosevelt was a leader and a statesman, a scholar and a politician. Beginning in 1933, he served as president until his death in 1945, and the general public knows much about this time in his life, with the exception of his poor health, of course, which he kept carefully hidden. Franklin D. Roosevelt is the only president to have served for three consecutive terms, and voted in for a fourth, a fact that allows him to stand out among the long list of American presidents. Notable events during his presidency include the end of the banking crisis; the enacting of the Federal Housing Administration, the Federal Communications Commission, and the Social Security Act; the long epidemic that was World War II; Roosevelt's "Four Freedoms" speech; the Lend-Lease Act with the

United Kingdom and the Soviet Union; and the Yalta Conference, among many others.[cccx]

Outside of his role as president of the United States, Franklin D. Roosevelt lived a full life. He was a father and a son, a husband and a career man. He was a bank officer and attended prestigious universities—Harvard University and Columbia University Law School—before practicing law. Additionally, he served as vice president for the Fidelity and Deposit Company. Perhaps most famously, Roosevelt served as governor of New York and president of the United States while he suffered from polio. Instead of allowing the disease to keep him from living a full life, he went above and beyond, training himself to walk without the power of his legs so that his voters would not know that he suffered in any capacity. What this book aims to do is determine who Franklin D. Roosevelt was as a person outside of the spotlight. This book wants to answer questions about this man. How did he interact with his wife and family? What were his exploits and his vices? His favored hobbies?

The following is an outline of Franklin D. Roosevelt's life that not only gives a brief overview of his best-known feats but also provides a glimpse into who he was as a person. In his inaugural address, Roosevelt said, "This nation asks for action, and action now," and he delivered until his last written words: "The only limit to our realization of tomorrow will be our doubts of today. Let us move forward with strong and active faith."

Chapter One: Childhood and Education

On January 30, 1882, Franklin Delano Roosevelt, named for his mother's uncle Franklin Hughes Delano, [cccxi] was born the only child of James Roosevelt and Sara Ann Delano in the Hudson Valley of Hyde Park, New York, at the Roosevelt estate that overlooked the Hudson River, seventy-five miles north of New York City. When his son was born, James Roosevelt wrote in Sara's diary: "At quarter to nine my Sallie had a splendid large boy, but was unconscious when he was born. Baby weighs ten pounds without clothes."[cccxii] For a moment, the family was in a tight spot. The mother and child came very close to dying, as the doctor administered too much chloroform due to Sara's intense labor pains. Franklin was not breathing at birth.

Soon overcoming the birth issues, Roosevelt grew up healthily in a privileged family. The estate had been in the family's possession for one hundred years. Both his parents derived from very wealthy and old New York families of English descent. American businessman and horse-breeder, James Roosevelt I worked primarily in the coal and transportation businesses, and he served as vice president for the Delaware and Hudson Railway and also served as president for the Southern Railway Security Company. As the inheritor of a good bit of wealth and a man who held a distaste for the business world, he retired early to the family estate and focused on his health, which was not always well. His family was Dutch, first appearing in America in 1654. Sara Ann Delano was James Roosevelt's second wife, and she devoted her life to caring for her son. Her family was Flemish and arrived in Massachusetts earlier than the Roosevelts appeared in New

York. Their families had close ties over the years. Franklin D. Roosevelt's parents were related long distance as sixth cousins.[cccxiii]

At the Roosevelt estate, Franklin spend most of his time with his mother; he grew up in a very patriarchal household. Sara was very protective of her son, while James was relatively absent, although biographer James MacGregor Burns notes that he was more involved than many of his fellow fathers.[cccxiv] Regardless, Roosevelt's mother remained his primary caretaker and influencer for his formative years, neglecting other life and wife duties. Over the years, she formed what some may consider an unhealthy relationship with her son and grew jealous of anyone who held his attention. First and foremost, she wanted to be the most important person in his life and shunned away others, including family. Sara is cited as saying, "My son Franklin is a Delano, not a Roosevelt at all."[cccxv]

As many of his status, Franklin did not lack the benefits of his family's privilege. As a five-year-old, Roosevelt visited the White House with his father where President Grover Cleveland told him, "I have one wish for you, little man, that you will never be president of the United States." Little did President Cleveland know that Franklin would hold the record for the most terms in office. In the summers, Roosevelt and his mother spent their days in Fairhaven, Massachusetts, at the Delano Homestead, and every year, Roosevelt's family would travel to Europe where he grew fluent in German and French and the family toured churches, museums, and palaces.[cccxvi],[cccxvii] During this time, Roosevelt began formulating opinions on other countries and their people. Franklin loved France, along with the people who lived there. On the other hand, he claimed that Germany and its citizens were rude and that they constantly said they were better than everyone else. There is a possibility that he inherited his opinions on Germany from his parents who thought that the people were "filthy … German swine."[cccxviii]

During his formative years, Roosevelt dabbled in many sports and hobbies. He learned to shoot, row, ride horses, and play lawn tennis and polo. In his teenage years, he took up golf and learned to sail.[cccxix] As befitting the son of a wealthy household, Roosevelt received a sailboat named *New Moon* from his father when he turned sixteen.[cccxx] In his early childhood, Roosevelt received his education at home from private tutors. During this time, he learned varying amounts of French, German, and Spanish, as this was the time that his family traveled often.

Many young men began their boarding schools at twelve, but that idea made Sara incredibly nervous. When he reached the age that his mother considered appropriate, which was fourteen years old, Franklin enrolled in an Episcopal boarding school, Groton School, in Groton, Massachusetts, known as the "bastion of the elite," and he learned alongside students from many other wealthy families.[cccxxi] In fact, ninety percent of the attendees were on the social register, a United States document, now outdated, that provides a directory of prominent American families. The document includes members of the social elite who lived within the boundaries of the American upper class, those of "old money" who identify as White Anglo-Saxon Protestants (WASPs).

Here at Groton, Franklin formed a bond with Endicott Peabody, the headmaster who encouraged Christians to engage public service and provide assistance to those less fortunate than them. He said, "If some Groton boys do not enter political life and do something for our land, it won't be because they have not been urged."[cccxxii] Peabody was a champion of independent thought, stating that he held no opinions but instead upheld his beliefs, which he claimed were always true and beyond question.[cccxxiii] Of Peabody, Roosevelt later said, "It was a blessing in my life to have the privilege of [his] guiding hand."[cccxxiv] He went as far as to write Peabody a letter after gaining presidency, saying, "For all that you have been and are to me I owe a debt of gratitude."[cccxxv] Peabody remained in Franklin's life, serving as the officiate at his wedding and paying a visit to Roosevelt during his presidency.[cccxxvi]

Although he formed a great bond with the headmaster, Franklin gained little attention while in school. The other students thought he was showy, too eager to gain teachers' attentions. In an attempt to fit in, Franklin purposely garnered demerits in the classroom for small offenses, such as whispering during class time.[cccxxvii] His best work was elsewhere, though. While Franklin did not excel in baseball, he stood out as an excellent manager, which helped his leadership skills flourish. In addition, he was a good orator, which allowed him to go far in the debating society. Peabody claimed that Roosevelt was "a quiet, satisfactory boy of more than ordinary intelligence, taking a good position in his form but not brilliant."[cccxxviii] Recalling little about him that stood out, another classmate said he was "nice, but completely colorless."[cccxxix] What others did notice was that Roosevelt was the only student who self-identified as a Democrat, which followed a family tradition.

Along with many of his classmates, Franklin began Harvard College in 1900 in Cambridge, Massachusetts,[cccxxx] where he joined the Alpha Delta Phi fraternity[cccxxxi] and the Fly Club,[cccxxxii] along with the Signet Society and the Hasty Pudding Club. He majored in history and political science while in college but showed no express interest in college work itself, and often cut classes. In fact, he escaped out a window during one lecture and climbed down a fire escape while the professor had his attention elsewhere. Therefore, he kept a "gentleman's C" in most classes, which means that he barely managed to pass. Just as at Groton, Roosevelt's classmates at Harvard held various opinions on him. One of his cousins, Alice, said, "He was a good little mother's boy whose friends were dull, who belonged to the minor clubs, and who never was at the really gay parties."[cccxxxiii] In light of such, Franklin had to earn his name elsewhere.

Roosevelt gained the titles of president and editor of *The Harvard Crimson*, Harvard's daily newspaper, during his last year. In this position, he learned leadership and responsibility while developing a taste for ambition. The staff members said that he was "a king of frictionless command," a trait that followed Roosevelt throughout the rest of his life.[cccxxxiv]

Looking back on his classes, Roosevelt said, "I took economics courses in college for four years, and everything I was taught was wrong."[cccxxxv] He graduated in 1903 with a Bachelor of Arts degree in history. In 1904, Roosevelt gained entry into Columbia Law School but decided to quit in 1907 after he passed the New York State Bar exam. In 1929, Franklin received an honorary LL.D. from Harvard,[cccxxxvi] and he received a posthumous J.D. from Columbia Law School.[cccxxxvii]

Continue reading!

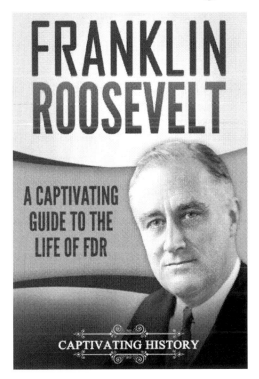

Check out this book!

Free Bonus from Captivating History (Available for a Limited time)

Hi History Lovers!

Now you have a chance to join our exclusive history list so you can get your first history ebook for free as well as discounts and a potential to get more history books for free! Simply visit the link below to join.

Captivatinghistory.com/ebook

Also, make sure to follow us on:

Twitter: @Captivhistory

Facebook: Captivating History: @captivatinghistory

Primary and Secondary Sources

---

[i] *The Gallop Poll 1999*. Wilmington, Delaware: Scholarly Resources Inc. 1999. pp. 248–249.

[ii] Reeves, Richard. *President Kennedy: Profile of Power.* 1993.

[iii] Reeves, Richard. *President Kennedy: Profile of Power.* 1993.

[iv] "John F. Kennedy and Ireland." *John F. Kennedy Presidential Library and Museum.* https://www.jfklibrary.org/JFK/JFK-in-History/John-F-Kennedy-and-Ireland.aspx. Accessed 18 August 2017.

[v] O'Brien, Michael. *John F. Kennedy: A Biography.* 2005.

[vi] Failla, Zak. "Looking Back on JFK's Time in Bronxville." *The Daily Voice.* 18 November 2013.

[vii] Dallek, Robert. *An Unfinished Life: John F. Kennedy, 1917—1963.* 2003.

[viii] Kenney, Charles. *John F. Kennedy: The Presidential Portfolio.* 2000.

[ix] Dallek, Robert. "The Medical Ordeals of JFK." *The Atlantic.* December 2002. https://web.archive.org/web/20160811195843/http://www.theatlantic.com/magazine/archive/2002/12/the-medical-ordeals-of-jfk/305572/?single_page=true. 24 August 2017.

[x] Kenney, Charles. *John F. Kennedy: The Presidential Portfolio.* 2000.

[xi] Dallek, Robert. *An Unfinished Life: John F. Kennedy, 1917—1963.* 2003.

[xii] Barkhorn, Eleanor. "JFK's Very Revealing Harvard Application Essay." *The Atlantic.* 21 November 2013. https://www.theatlantic.com/education/archive/2013/11/jfks-very-revealing-harvard-application-essay/281699/. 25 August 2017.

[xiii] Clarke, John. "Selling J.F.K.'s Boat." *The New Yorker.* 19 May 2015.

[xiv] Dallek, Robert. *An Unfinished Life: John F. Kennedy, 1917—1963.* 2003.

[xv] Dallek, Robert. *An Unfinished Life: John F. Kennedy, 1917—1963.* 2003.

[xvi] Dallek, Robert. *An Unfinished Life: John F. Kennedy, 1917—1963.* 2003.

[xvii] Brinkley, Alan. *John F. Kennedy.* 2012.

[xviii] Kenney, Charles. *John F. Kennedy: The Presidential Portfolio.* 2000.

[xix] Kenney, Charles. *John F. Kennedy: The Presidential Portfolio.* 2000.

[xx] Dallek, Robert. *An Unfinished Life: John F. Kennedy, 1917—1963.* 2003.

[xxi] Dallek, Robert. "The Medical Ordeals of JFK." *The Atlantic.* December 2002. https://web.archive.org/web/20160811195843/http://www.theatlantic.com/magazine/archive/2002/12/the-medical-ordeals-of-jfk/305572/?single_page=true. 24 August 2017.

[xxii] Mandel, Lee R. "Endocrine and Autoimmune Aspects of the Health History of John F. Kennedy." *Annals of Internal Medicine.* 1 September 2009. http://annals.org/aim/article/744707/endocrine-

autoimmune-aspects-health-history-john-f-kennedy#xref-ref-9-1. 1 September 2017.

[xxiii] Mandel, Lee R. "Endocrine and Autoimmune Aspects of the Health History of John F. Kennedy." *Annals of Internal Medicine*. 1 September 2009. http://annals.org/aim/article/744707/endocrine-autoimmune-aspects-health-history-john-f-kennedy#xref-ref-9-1. 1 September 2017.

[xxiv] Kempe, Frederick. *Berlin 1961*. 2012.

[xxv] Reeves, Richard. *President Kennedy: Profile of Power*. 1993.

[xxvi] Reeves, Richard. *President Kennedy: Profile of Power*. 1993.

[xxvii] Dallek, Robert. *An Unfinished Life: John F. Kennedy, 1917—1963*. 2003.

[xxviii] Osborne, Robert. *Leading Ladies: The 50 Most Unforgettable Actresses of the Studio Era*. 2006.

[xxix] Dallek, Robert. *An Unfinished Life: John F. Kennedy, 1917—1963*. 2003.

[xxx] Reeves, Richard. *President Kennedy: Profile of Power*. 1993.

[xxxi] Reeves, Richard. *President Kennedy: Profile of Power*. 1993.

[xxxii] Donovan, Robert J. *PT-109: John F. Kennedy in WW II*. 2001.

[xxxiii] Donovan, Robert J. *PT-109: John F. Kennedy in WW II*. 2001.

[xxxiv] O'Brien, Michael. *John F. Kennedy: A Biography*. 2005.

[xxxv] Dallek, Robert. *An Unfinished Life: John F. Kennedy, 1917—1963*. 2003.

[xxxvi] Dallek, Robert. *An Unfinished Life: John F. Kennedy, 1917—1963*. 2003.

[xxxvii] Brinkley, Alan. *John F. Kennedy*. 2012.

[xxxviii] Brinkley, Alan. *John F. Kennedy*. 2012.

xxxix O'Brien, Michael. *John F. Kennedy: A Biography*. 2005.

xl O'Brien, Michael. *John F. Kennedy: A Biography*. 2005.

xli Brinkley, Alan. *John F. Kennedy*. 2012.

xlii Brinkley, Alan. *John F. Kennedy*. 2012.

xliii Brinkley, Alan. *John F. Kennedy*. 2012.

xliv Brinkley, Alan. *John F. Kennedy*. 2012.

xlv Reeves, Richard. *President Kennedy: Profile of Power*. 1993.

xlvi Reeves, Richard. *President Kennedy: Profile of Power*. 1993.

xlvii Kempe, Frederick. *Berlin 1961*. 2011.

xlviii Reeves, Richard. *President Kennedy: Profile of Power*. 1993.

xlix Reeves, Richard. *President Kennedy: Profile of Power*. 1993.

l Reeves, Richard. *President Kennedy: Profile of Power*. 1993.

li Reeves, Richard. *President Kennedy: Profile of Power*. 1993.

lii Reeves, Richard. *President Kennedy: Profile of Power*. 1993.

liii Schlesinger, Jr., Arthur M. *A Thousand Days: John F. Kennedy in the White House*. 2002.

liv Reeves, Richard. *President Kennedy: Profile of Power*. 1993.

lv Schlesinger, Jr., Arthur M. *A Thousand Days: John F. Kennedy in the White House*. 2002.

lvi Reeves, Richard. *President Kennedy: Profile of Power*. 1993.

lvii Reeves, Richard. *President Kennedy: Profile of Power*. 1993.

lviii Reeves, Richard. *President Kennedy: Profile of Power*. 1993.

lix Reeves, Richard. *President Kennedy: Profile of Power*. 1993.

lx Reeves, Richard. *President Kennedy: Profile of Power*. 1993.

[lxi] Reeves, Richard. *President Kennedy: Profile of Power.* 1993.

[lxii] Reeves, Richard. *President Kennedy: Profile of Power.* 1993.

[lxiii] Kenney, Charles. *John F. Kennedy: The Presidential Portfolio.* 2000.

[lxiv] Reeves, Richard. *President Kennedy: Profile of Power.* 1993.

[lxv] Schlesinger, Jr., Arthur M. *A Thousand Days: John F. Kennedy in the White House.* 2002.

[lxvi] Reeves, Richard. *President Kennedy: Profile of Power.* 1993.

[lxvii] Reeves, Richard. *President Kennedy: Profile of Power.* 1993.

[lxviii] Dallek, Robert. *An Unfinished Life: John F. Kennedy, 1917—1963.* 2003.

[lxix] Schlesinger, Jr., Arthur M. *A Thousand Days: John F. Kennedy in the White House.* 2002.

[lxx] Meisler, Stanley. *When the World Calls: The Inside Story of the Peace Corps and Its First Fifty Years.* 2011.

[lxxi] Reeves, Richard. *President Kennedy: Profile of Power.* 1993.

[lxxii] Reeves, Richard. *President Kennedy: Profile of Power.* 1993.

[lxxiii] Dunnigan, James, and Albert Nofi. *Dirty Little Secrets of the Vietnam War.* 1999.

[lxxiv] Reeves, Richard. *President Kennedy: Profile of Power.* 1993.

[lxxv] Reeves, Richard. *President Kennedy: Profile of Power.* 1993.

[lxxvi] Reeves, Richard. *President Kennedy: Profile of Power.* 1993.

[lxxvii] Reeves, Richard. *President Kennedy: Profile of Power.* 1993.

[lxxviii] Reeves, Richard. *President Kennedy: Profile of Power.* 1993.

[lxxix] Reeves, Richard. *President Kennedy: Profile of Power.* 1993.

[lxxx] Reeves, Richard. *President Kennedy: Profile of Power.* 1993.

[lxxxi] Reeves, Richard. *President Kennedy: Profile of Power.* 1993.

[lxxxii] Reeves, Richard. *President Kennedy: Profile of Power.* 1993.

[lxxxiii] Reeves, Richard. *President Kennedy: Profile of Power.* 1993.

[lxxxiv] Reeves, Richard. *President Kennedy: Profile of Power.* 1993.

[lxxxv] Talbot, David. "Warrior for Peace." *Time Magazine.* 21 June 2007.

[lxxxvi] Matthews, Chris. *Jack Kennedy: Elusive Hero.* 2011.

[lxxxvii] Sorensen, Theodore. *Kennedy.* 1965.

[lxxxviii] Reeves, Richard. *President Kennedy: Profile of Power.* 1993.

[lxxxix] Reeves, Richard. *President Kennedy: Profile of Power.* 1993

[xc] Dallek, Robert. *An Unfinished Life: John F. Kennedy, 1917—1963.* 2003.

[xci] Reeves, Richard. *President Kennedy: Profile of Power.* 1993

[xcii] Walt, Stephen M. *The Origins of Alliances.* 1987.

[xciii] Salt, Jeremey. *The Unmaking of the Middle East: A History of Western Disorder in Arab Lands.* 2008.

[xciv] Salt, Jeremey. *The Unmaking of the Middle East: A History of Western Disorder in Arab Lands.* 2008.

[xcv] Hersh, Seymour. *The Dark Side of Camelot.* 1997.

[xcvi] Salt, Jeremey. *The Unmaking of the Middle East: A History of Western Disorder in Arab Lands.* 2008.

[xcvii] Salt, Jeremey. *The Unmaking of the Middle East: A History of Western Disorder in Arab Lands.* 2008.

[xcviii] Hersh, Seymour. *The Dark Side of Camelot.* 1997.

[xcix] Trachtenberg, Marc. *A Constructed Peace: The Making of the European Settlement, 1945—1963.* 8 February 1999.

[c] Gibson, Bryan R. *Sold Out? US Foreign Policy, Iraq, the Kurds, and the Cold War*. 2015.

[ci] Gibson, Bryan R. *Sold Out? US Foreign Policy, Iraq, the Kurds, and the Cold War*. 2015.

[cii] Gibson, Bryan R. *Sold Out? US Foreign Policy, Iraq, the Kurds, and the Cold War*. 2015.

[ciii] Reeves, Richard. *President Kennedy: Profile of Power*. 1993

[civ] Frum, David. *How We Got Here: The '70s*. 2000.

[cv] Frum, David. *How We Got Here: The '70s*. 2000.

[cvi] Reeves, Richard. *President Kennedy: Profile of Power*. 1993.

[cvii] O'Brien, Michael. *John F. Kennedy: A Biography*. 2005.

[cviii] Reeves, Richard. *President Kennedy: Profile of Power*. 1993.

[cix] Reeves, Richard. *President Kennedy: Profile of Power*. 1993.

[cx] Grantham. *The Life and Death of the Solid South: A Political History*. 1988.

[cxi] Dallek, Robert. *An Unfinished Life: John F. Kennedy, 1917—1963*. 2003.

[cxii] Dallek, Robert. *An Unfinished Life: John F. Kennedy, 1917—1963*. 2003.

[cxiii] Brauer, Carl M. "John F. Kennedy." *The Presidents: A Reference History*. edited by Henry Graff. 2002.

[cxiv] Brauer, Carl M. "John F. Kennedy." *The Presidents: A Reference History*. edited by Henry Graff. 2002.

[cxv] Bryant, Nick. "Black Man Who Was Crazy Enough to Apply to Ole Miss." *The Journal of Blacks in Higher Education*. Autumn 2006.

[cxvi] Brauer, Carl M. "John F. Kennedy." *The Presidents: A Reference History*. edited by Henry Graff. 2002.

cxvii Reeves, Richard. *President Kennedy: Profile of Power.* 1993.

cxviii Brauer, Carl M. "John F. Kennedy." *The Presidents: A Reference History.* edited by Henry Graff. 2002.

cxix Bryant, Nick. "Black Man Who Was Crazy Enough to Apply to Ole Miss." *The Journal of Blacks in Higher Education.* Autumn 2006.

cxx Dallek, Robert. *An Unfinished Life: John F. Kennedy, 1917—1963.* 2003.

cxxi Reeves, Richard. *President Kennedy: Profile of Power.* 1993.

cxxii Reeves, Richard. *President Kennedy: Profile of Power.* 1993.

cxxiii Reeves, Richard. *President Kennedy: Profile of Power.* 1993.

cxxiv Schlesinger, Jr., Arthur M. *A Thousand Days: John F. Kennedy in the White House.* 2002.

cxxv Cohen, Andrew. *Two Days in June: John F. Kennedy and the 48 Hours That Changed History.* 2014.

cxxvi Goduti, Jr., Philip A. *Robert F. Kennedy and the Shaping of Civil Rights, 1960-1964.* 2012.

cxxvii Reeves, Richard. *President Kennedy: Profile of Power.* 1993.

cxxviii Reeves, Richard. *President Kennedy: Profile of Power.* 1993.

cxxix Reeves, Richard. *President Kennedy: Profile of Power.* 1993.

cxxx Brauer, Carl M. "John F. Kennedy." *The Presidents: A Reference History.* edited by Henry Graff. 2002.

cxxxi Reeves, Richard. *President Kennedy: Profile of Power.* 1993.

cxxxii Dallek, Robert. *An Unfinished Life: John F. Kennedy, 1917—1963.* 2003.

cxxxiii Reeves, Richard. *President Kennedy: Profile of Power.* 1993.

cxxxiv Dallek, Robert. *An Unfinished Life: John F. Kennedy, 1917—1963.* 2003.

cxxxv Brauer, Carl M. "John F. Kennedy." *The Presidents: A Reference History.* edited by Henry Graff. 2002.

cxxxvi Salinger, Pierre. *John F. Kennedy: Commander in Chief: A Profile in Leadership.* 1997.

cxxxvii Andersen, Christopher. The Good Son: JFK Jr. and the Mother He Loved. 2015.

cxxxviii Schlesinger, Arthur. Robert Kennedy and His Times, Volume 2. 2002.

cxxxix Adler, Bill. The Eloquent Jacqueline Kennedy Onassis: A Portrait in Her Own Words. 2009.

cxl Leaming, Barbara. Jacqueline Bouvier Kennedy Onassis: The Untold Story. 2014.

cxli "Life of Jacqueline B. Kennedy." John F. Kennedy Presidential Library and Museum." https://www.jfklibrary.org/JFK/Life-of-Jacqueline-B-Kennedy.aspx. Accessed 9 August 2017.

cxlii Tracy, Kathleen. The Everything Jacqueline Kennedy Onassis Book: A Portrait of an American Icon. 2008.

cxliii Tracy, Kathleen. The Everything Jacqueline Kennedy Onassis Book: A Portrait of an American Icon. 2008.

cxliv "Life of Jacqueline B. Kennedy." John F. Kennedy Presidential Library and Museum." https://www.jfklibrary.org/JFK/Life-of-Jacqueline-B-Kennedy.aspx. Accessed 9 August 2017.

cxlv Adler, Bill. The Eloquent Jacqueline Kennedy Onassis: A Portrait in Her Own Words. 2009.

cxlvi Adler, Bill. The Eloquent Jacqueline Kennedy Onassis: A Portrait in Her Own Words. 2009.

cxlvii Pottker, Jan. Janet and Jackie: The Story of a Mother and Her Daughter, Jacqueline Kennedy Onassis. 2002.

cxlviii "Life of Jacqueline B. Kennedy." John F. Kennedy: Presidential Library and Museum. https://www.jfklibrary.org/JFK/Life-of-Jacqueline-B-Kennedy.aspx. Accessed 24 July 2017.

cxlix "Life of Jacqueline B. Kennedy." John F. Kennedy: Presidential Library and Museum. https://www.jfklibrary.org/JFK/Life-of-Jacqueline-B-Kennedy.aspx. Accessed 24 July 2017.

cl Harris, Bill. First Ladies Fact Book—Revised and Updated: The Childhoods, Courtships, Marriages, Campaigns, Accomplishments, and Legacies of Every First Lady from Martha Washington to Michelle Obama. 2012.

cli Hunt, Amber, and David Batcher. Kennedy Wives: Triumph and Tragedy in America's Most Public Family. 2014.

clii Badrun Alam, Mohammed. Jackie Kennedy: Trailblazer. 2006.

cliii Hunt, Amber, and David Batcher. Kennedy Wives: Triumph and Tragedy in America's Most Public Family. 2014.

cliv Hunt, Amber, and David Batcher. Kennedy Wives: Triumph and Tragedy in America's Most Public Family. 2014.

clv Hunt, Amber, and David Batcher. Kennedy Wives: Triumph and Tragedy in America's Most Public Family. 2014.

clvi McFadden, Robert D. "Death of a First Lady: Jacqueline Kennedy Onassis Dies of Cancer at 64." New York Times. 20 May 1994. http://www.nytimes.com/learning/general/onthisday/bday/0728.html. Accessed 24 July 2017.

clvii Tracy, Kathleen. The Everything Jacqueline Kennedy Onassis Book: A Portrait of an American Icon. 2008.

clviii Pottker, Jan. Janet and Jackie: The Story of a Mother and Her Daughter, Jacqueline Kennedy Onassis. 2002.

clix Adler, Bill. The Eloquent Jacqueline Kennedy Onassis: A Portrait in Her Own Words. 2009.

clx Adler, Bill. The Eloquent Jacqueline Kennedy Onassis: A Portrait in Her Own Words. 2009.

clxi Spoto, Donald. Jacqueline Bouvier Kennedy Onassis: A Life. 2000.

clxii Spoto, Donald. Jacqueline Bouvier Kennedy Onassis: A Life. 2000.

clxiii Adler, Bill. The Eloquent Jacqueline Kennedy Onassis: A Portrait in Her Own Words. 2009.

clxiv Adler, Bill. The Eloquent Jacqueline Kennedy Onassis: A Portrait in Her Own Words. 2009.

clxv Spoto, Donald. Jacqueline Bouvier Kennedy Onassis: A Life. 2000.

clxvi Leaming, Barbara. Mrs. Kennedy: The Missing History of the Kennedy Years. 2001.

clxvii Hunt, Amber, and David Batcher. Kennedy Wives: Triumph and Tragedy in America's Most Public Family. 2014.

clxviii Adler, Bill. The Eloquent Jacqueline Kennedy Onassis: A Portrait in Her Own Words. 2009.

clxix Adler, Bill. The Eloquent Jacqueline Kennedy Onassis: A Portrait in Her Own Words. 2009.

clxx "Life of Jacqueline B. Kennedy." John F. Kennedy Presidential Library and Museum." https://www.jfklibrary.org/JFK/Life-of-Jacqueline-B-Kennedy.aspx. Accessed 9 August 2017.

clxxi Adler, Bill. The Eloquent Jacqueline Kennedy Onassis: A Portrait in Her Own Words. 2009.

clxxii Leaming, Barbara. Jacqueline Bouvier Kennedy Onassis: The Untold Story. 2014.

clxxiii Leaming, Barbara. Jacqueline Bouvier Kennedy Onassis: The Untold Story. 2014.

clxxiv McFadden, Robert D. "Death of a First Lady: Jacqueline Kennedy Onassis Dies of Cancer at 64." New York Times. 20 May 1994.

clxxv Adler, Bill. The Eloquent Jacqueline Kennedy Onassis: A Portrait in Her Own Words. 2009.

clxxvi Adler, Bill. The Eloquent Jacqueline Kennedy Onassis: A Portrait in Her Own Words. 2009.

clxxvii Adler, Bill. The Eloquent Jacqueline Kennedy Onassis: A Portrait in Her Own Words. 2009.

clxxviii Spoto, Donald. Jacqueline Bouvier Kennedy Onassis: A Life. 2000.

clxxix Hunt, Amber, and David Batcher. Kennedy Wives: Triumph and Tragedy in America's Most Public Family. 2014.

clxxx Badrun Alam, Mohammed. Jackie Kennedy: Trailblazer. 2006.

clxxxi Harris, Bill. First Ladies Fact Book—Revised and Updated: The Childhoods, Courtships, Marriages, Campaigns, Accomplishments, and Legacies of Every First Lady from Martha Washington to Michelle Obama. 2012.

clxxxii "Wedding of Jacqueline Bouvier and John F. Kennedy, Newport, Rhode Island, September 12, 1953." John F. Kennedy Presidential Library and Museum. https://www.jfklibrary.org/Research/Research-Aids/Ready-Reference/JKO-Fast-Facts/Wedding-Details.aspx. Accessed 27 July 2017.

clxxxiii Badrun Alam, Mohammed. Jackie Kennedy: Trailblazer. 2006.

clxxxiv Dallek, Robert. An Unfinished Life: John F. Kennedy, 1917—1963. 2004.

clxxxv Badrun Alam, Mohammed. Jackie Kennedy: Trailblazer. 2006.

clxxxvi Badrun Alam, Mohammed. Jackie Kennedy: Trailblazer. 2006.

clxxxvii Hunt, Amber, and David Batcher. Kennedy Wives: Triumph and Tragedy in America's Most Public Family. 2014.

clxxxviii Badrun Alam, Mohammed. Jackie Kennedy: Trailblazer. 2006.

clxxxix Andersen, Christopher. The Good Son: JFK Jr. and the Mother He Loved. 2015.

cxc Andersen, Christopher. The Good Son: JFK Jr. and the Mother He Loved. 2015.

cxci Andersen, Christopher. The Good Son: JFK Jr. and the Mother He Loved. 2015.

cxcii Andersen, Christopher. The Good Son: JFK Jr. and the Mother He Loved. 2015.

cxciii Andersen, Christopher. The Good Son: JFK Jr. and the Mother He Loved. 2015.

cxciv Beschloss, Michael. Historical Conversations on Life with John F. Kennedy. 2011.

cxcv Schlesinger, Arthur M., Jr. A Thousand Days: John F. Kennedy in the White House. 1965.

cxcvi Leaming, Barbara. Jacqueline Bouvier Kennedy Onassis: The Untold Story. 2014.

cxcvii Andersen, Christopher. The Good Son: JFK Jr. and the Mother He Loved. 2015.

cxcviii "Why Jackie Kennedy was the Original Modern Mom." People. 6 July 2015. http://people.com/celebrity/jackie-kennedy-and-her-children-the-former-first-lady-was-a-modern-mom/. Accessed 1 August 2017.

cxcix Adler, Bill. The Eloquent Jacqueline Kennedy Onassis: A Portrait in Her Own Words. 2009.

cc "Why Jackie Kennedy was the Original Modern Mom." People. 6 July 2015. http://people.com/celebrity/jackie-kennedy-and-her-children-the-former-first-lady-was-a-modern-mom/. Accessed 1 August 2017.

cci Adler, Bill. The Eloquent Jacqueline Kennedy Onassis: A Portrait in Her Own Words. 2009.

ccii "Why Jackie Kennedy was the Original Modern Mom." People. 6 July 2015. http://people.com/celebrity/jackie-kennedy-and-her-children-the-former-first-lady-was-a-modern-mom/. Accessed 1 August 2017.

cciii "Why Jackie Kennedy was the Original Modern Mom." People. 6 July 2015. http://people.com/celebrity/jackie-kennedy-and-her-children-the-former-first-lady-was-a-modern-mom/. Accessed 1 August 2017.

cciv "Why Jackie Kennedy was the Original Modern Mom." People. 6 July 2015. http://people.com/celebrity/jackie-kennedy-and-her-children-the-former-first-lady-was-a-modern-mom/. Accessed 1 August 2017.

ccv Andersen, Christopher. The Good Son: JFK Jr. and the Mother He Loved. 2015.

ccvi Badrun Alam, Mohammed. Jackie Kennedy: Trailblazer. 2006.

ccvii Hunt, Amber, and David Batcher. Kennedy Wives: Triumph and Tragedy in America's Most Public Family. 2014.

ccviii Wertheime, Molly Meijer. Inventing a Voice: The Rhetoric of American First Ladies of the Twentieth Century. 2004.

ccix Andersen, Christopher. The Good Son: JFK Jr. and the Mother He Loved. 2015.

ccx Andersen, Christopher. The Good Son: JFK Jr. and the Mother He Loved. 2015.

ccxi "Life of Jacqueline B. Kennedy." John F. Kennedy: Presidential Library and Museum. https://www.jfklibrary.org/JFK/Life-of-Jacqueline-B-Kennedy.aspx. Accessed 24 July 2017.

ccxii Beasley, Maurine. First Ladies and the Press: The Unfinished Partnership of the Media Age. 2005.

ccxiii Beasley, Maurine. First Ladies and the Press: The Unfinished Partnership of the Media Age. 2005.

ccxiv Tina Flaherty. What Jackie Taught Us: Lessons from the Remarkable Life of Jacqueline. 2004.

ccxv Beasley, Maurine. First Ladies and the Press: The Unfinished Partnership of the Media Age. 2005.

ccxvi Adler, Bill. The Eloquent Jacqueline Kennedy Onassis: A Portrait in Her Own Words. 2009.

ccxvii Adler, Bill. The Eloquent Jacqueline Kennedy Onassis: A Portrait in Her Own Words. 2009.

ccxviii Beasley, Maurine. First Ladies and the Press: The Unfinished Partnership of the Media Age. 2005.

ccxix Hunt, Amber, and David Batcher. Kennedy Wives: Triumph and Tragedy in America's Most Public Family. 2014.

ccxx "Return of the Jackie Look-Sort of Fashion from A-Line Dresses to Fitted Jackets." Newsweek. 28 August 1994. http://www.newsweek.com/return-jackie-look-sort-fashion-line-dresses-fitted-jackets-187932. Accessed 9 August 2017.

ccxxi Hunt, Amber, and David Batcher. Kennedy Wives: Triumph and Tragedy in America's Most Public Family. 2014.

ccxxii Beasley, Maurine. First Ladies and the Press: The Unfinished Partnership of the Media Age. 2005.

ccxxiii Hunt, Amber, and David Batcher. Kennedy Wives: Triumph and Tragedy in America's Most Public Family. 2014.

ccxxiv Beasley, Maurine. First Ladies and the Press: The Unfinished Partnership of the Media Age. 2005.

ccxxv Schwalbe, Carol B. "Jacqueline Kennedy and Cold War Propaganda." Journal of Broadcasting and Electronic Media. 2005.

ccxxvi Beasley, Maurine. First Ladies and the Press: The Unfinished Partnership of the Media Age. 2005.

ccxxvii "Jacqueline Kennedy in the White House." The John F. Kennedy Presidential Library and Museum. https://www.jfklibrary.org/JFK/JFK-in-History/Jacqueline-Kennedy-in-the-White-House.aspx. Accessed 2 August 2017.

ccxxviii "Jacqueline Kennedy in the White House." The John F. Kennedy Presidential Library and Museum. https://www.jfklibrary.org/JFK/JFK-in-History/Jacqueline-Kennedy-in-the-White-House.aspx. Accessed 2 August 2017.

ccxxix "Jacqueline Kennedy in the White House." The John F. Kennedy Presidential Library and Museum. https://www.jfklibrary.org/JFK/JFK-in-History/Jacqueline-Kennedy-in-the-White-House.aspx. Accessed 2 August 2017.

ccxxx "Jacqueline Kennedy in the White House." The John F. Kennedy Presidential Library and Museum. https://www.jfklibrary.org/JFK/JFK-in-History/Jacqueline-Kennedy-in-the-White-House.aspx. Accessed 2 August 2017.

ccxxxi Abbott, James, and Elaine Rice. Designing Camelot: The Kennedy White House Restoration. 1997.

ccxxxii Abbott, James, and Elaine Rice. Designing Camelot: The Kennedy White House Restoration. 1997.

ccxxxiii "Jacqueline Kennedy in the White House." The John F. Kennedy Presidential Library and Museum. https://www.jfklibrary.org/JFK/JFK-in-History/Jacqueline-Kennedy-in-the-White-House.aspx. Accessed 2 August 2017.

ccxxxiv "Little-Known Facts About Our First Ladies." National First Ladies' Library. http://www.firstladies.org/facinatingfacts.aspx. Accessed 2 August 2017.

ccxxxv Beasley, Maurine. First Ladies and the Press: The Unfinished Partnership of the Media Age. 2005.

ccxxxvi Goodman, Jon, Hugh Sidey, and Letitia Baldridge. The Kennedy Mystique: Creating Camelot: Essays. 2006.

ccxxxvii "Nation: La Presidente." Time. http://content.time.com/time/magazine/article/0,9171,938093,00.html. Accessed 2 August 2017.

ccxxxviii Blair, W. Grainger. "Just an Escort, Kennedy Jokes as Wife's Charm Enchants Paris; First Lady Wins Bouquets From Press—She Also Has Brief Chance to Visit Museum and Admire Manet." The New York Times. 3 June 2961. http://query.nytimes.com/gst/abstract.html?res=9403E4DE1730EE32A25750C0A9609C946091D6CF&legacy=true. Accessed 2 August 2017.

ccxxxix "First Lady Biography: Jackie Kennedy." National First Ladies' Library. http://www.firstladies.org/biographies/firstladies.aspx?biography=36. Accessed 2 August 2017.

ccxl Meagher, Michael, and Larry D. Gragg. John F. Kennedy: A Biography. 2011.

ccxli "Jackie Kennedy Adopts Sardar, March 23, 1962." Politico. 23 March 2011. http://www.politico.com/story/2011/03/jackie-kennedy-adopts-sardar-march-23-1962-051743. 7 August 2017.

ccxlii Glass, Andrew. "Jacqueline Kennedy Begins South Asia Trip, March 12, 1962." Politico. 12 March 2015. http://www.politico.com/story/2015/03/this-day-in-politics-march-12-1962-115982. Accessed 7 August 2017.

ccxliii Bugliosi, Vincent. Four Days in November: The Assassination of John F. Kennedy. 2007.

ccxliv "Selections from Lady Bird's Diary on the Assassination." Lady Bird Johnson: Portrait of a First Lady. 22 November 1963. http://www.pbs.org/ladybird/epicenter/epicenter_doc_diary.html. Accessed 7 August 2017.

ccxlv "Testimony of Clinton J. Hill, Special Agent, Secret Service." Warren Commission Hearings. http://www.aarclibrary.org/publib/jfk/wc/wcvols/wh2/html/WC_Vol2_0070b.htm. Accessed 7 August 2017.

ccxlvi "Mrs. John F. Kennedy." Warren Commission Hearings, Volume V." http://www.maryferrell.org/showDoc.html?docId=40&relPageId=190. Accessed 7 August 2017.

ccxlvii "Selections from Lady Bird's Diary on the Assassination." Lady Bird Johnson: Portrait of a First Lady. 22 November 1963. http://www.pbs.org/ladybird/epicenter/epicenter_doc_diary.html. Accessed 7 August 2017.

ccxlviii "Selections from Lady Bird's Diary on the Assassination." Lady Bird Johnson: Portrait of a First Lady. 22 November 1963. http://www.pbs.org/ladybird/epicenter/epicenter_doc_diary.html. Accessed 7 August 2017.

ccxlix "Selections from Lady Bird's Diary on the Assassination." Lady Bird Johnson: Portrait of a First Lady. 22 November 1963.

http://www.pbs.org/ladybird/epicenter/epicenter_doc_diary.html. Accessed 7 August 2017.

ccl "Selections from Lady Bird's Diary on the Assassination." Lady Bird Johnson: Portrait of a First Lady. 22 November 1963. http://www.pbs.org/ladybird/epicenter/epicenter_doc_diary.html. Accessed 7 August 2017.

ccli Caro, Robert. A. The Passage of Power: Volume 4 of The Years of Lyndon Johnson. 2013.

cclii Hilty, James. Robert Kennedy: Brother Protector. 2000.

ccliii Hunt, Amber, and David Batcher. Kennedy Wives: Triumph and Tragedy in America's Most Public Family. 2014.

ccliv Hunt, Amber, and David Batcher. Kennedy Wives: Triumph and Tragedy in America's Most Public Family. 2014.

cclv Lewis, Anthony. "Warren Commission Finds Oswald Guilty and Says Assassin and Ruby Acted Alone." The New York Times. 28 September 1964.

cclvi White, Theodore H. "For President Kennedy: An Epilogue." Life. 6 December 1963.

cclvii White, Theodore H. "For President Kennedy: An Epilogue." Life. 6 December 1963.

cclviii Andersen, Christopher. The Good Son: JFK Jr. and the Mother He Loved. 2015.

cclix Tracy, Kathleen. The Everything Jacqueline Kennedy Onassis Book: A Portrait of an American Icon. 2008.

cclx Badrul Alam, Mohammed. Jackie Kennedy: Trailblazer. 2006.

cclxi Little, Harriet Fitch. "Jacqueline Kennedy's Charm Offensive." The Phnom Penh Post. 21 March 2015.

cclxii Leaming, Barbara. Jacqueline Bouvier Kennedy Onassis: The Untold Story. 2014.

cclxiii Hersh, Burton. Edward Kennedy: An Intimate Biography. 2010.

cclxiv Spoto, Donald. Jacqueline Bouvier Kennedy Onassis: A Life. 2000.

cclxv Tracy, Kathleen. The Everything Jacqueline Kennedy Onassis Book: A Portrait of an American Icon. 2008.

cclxvi Heymann, C. David. American Legacy: The Story of John and Caroline Kennedy. 2007.

cclxvii Flynt, Larry, and David Eisenbach. One Nation Under Sex: How the Private Lives of Presidents, First Ladies and Their Lovers Changed the Course of American History. 2011.

cclxviii Morriss, John G. "Kennedy Claims Victory; and then Shots Ring Out." The New York Times. 6 June 1968. http://query.nytimes.com/gst/abstract.html?res=9404E1D91138E134BC4D53DFB0668383679EDE&legacy=true. Accessed 8 August 2017.

cclxix Hill, Gladwin. "Kennedy is Dead, Victim of Assassin; Suspect, Arab Immigrant, Arraigned' Johnson Appoints Panel on Violence." The New York Times. 6 June 1968. http://www.nytimes.com/learning/general/onthisday/big/0605.html#article. Accessed 8 August 2017.

cclxx Seely, Katherine. "John F. Kennedy Jr., Heir to a Formidable Dynasty." The New York Times. 19 July 1999. http://www.nytimes.com/1999/07/19/us/john-f-kennedy-jr-heir-to-a-formidable-dynasty.html?pagewanted=all. 8 August 2017.

cclxxi Hunt, Amber, and David Batcher. Kennedy Wives: Triumph and Tragedy in America's Most Public Family. 2014.

cclxxii Tracy, Kathleen. The Everything Jacqueline Kennedy Onassis Book: A Portrait of an American Icon. 2008.

~~cclxxiii Silverman, Al. The Time of Their Lives. 2008.~~

cclxxiv Reeves, Richard. Convention. 1977.

cclxxv Leaming, Barbara. Jacqueline Bouvier Kennedy Onassis: The Untold Story. 2014.

cclxxvi Lawrence, Greg. Jackie as Editor: The Literary Life of Jacqueline Kennedy Onassis. 2011.

cclxxvii Clinton, Hillary Rodham. Living History. 2003.

cclxxviii Lewis, Kathy. "Jacqueline Kennedy Onassis Reaches out to President Clinton—She Ends Long Political Isolation." Seattle Times Newspaper. 25 August 1993. http://community.seattletimes.nwsource.com/archive/?date=19930825&slug=1717693. Accessed 8 August 2017.

cclxxix Leaming, Barbara. Jacqueline Bouvier Kennedy Onassis: The Untold Story. 2014.

cclxxx Leaming, Barbara. Jacqueline Bouvier Kennedy Onassis: The Untold Story. 2014.

cclxxxi Leaming, Barbara. Jacqueline Bouvier Kennedy Onassis: The Untold Story. 2014.

cclxxxii Leaming, Barbara. Jacqueline Bouvier Kennedy Onassis: The Untold Story. 2014.

cclxxxiii Andersen, Christopher. The Good Son: JFK Jr. and the Mother He Loved. 2015.

cclxxxiv Bowles, Hamish. Jacqueline Kennedy: The White House Years: Selections from the John F. Kennedy Library and Museum. 2001.

cclxxxv "Return of the Jackie Look-Sort of Fashion from A-Line Dresses to Fitted Jackets." Newsweek. 28 August 1994. http://www.newsweek.com/return-jackie-look-sort-fashion-line-dresses-fitted-jackets-187932. Accessed 9 August 2017.

cclxxxvi Collins, Amy Fine. "It Had to be Kenneth." Vanity Fair. 1 June 2003. https://www.vanityfair.com/news/2003/06/kenneth-battelle-hairdresser-jackie-kennedy. Accessed 9 August 2017.

cclxxxvii "The International Best Dressed List: The International Hall of Fame: Women." Vanity Fair. 1965. https://web.archive.org/web/20130712215415/http://www.vanityfair.com/style/the-international-best-dressed-list/hall-of-fame-women. Accessed 9 August 2017.

cclxxxviii "Jacqueline Kennedy: The White House Years." Metropolitan Museum of Art. http://metmuseum.org/press/exhibitions/2000/jacqueline-kennedy-the-white-house-years. Accessed 9 August 2017.

cclxxxix Kifner, John. "Central Park Honor for Jacqueline Onassis." The New York Times. 23 July 1994.

ccxc "Send a New Year's Message to the Moon on Japan's SELENE Mission: Buzz Aldrin, Ray Bradbury, and More Have Wished Upon the Moon." The Planetary Society. 11 January 2007. http://www.planetary.org/press-room/releases/2007/0111_Send_a_New_Years_Message_to_the_Moon.html. 9 August 2017.

ccxci "The Nobel Prize in Literature 1953." The Official Website of the Nobel Prize. http://www.nobelprize.org/nobel_prizes/literature/laureates/1953/. Accessed 18 May 2017.

ccxcii "Sir Winston Churchill: A Chronology." Churchill College, Cambridge. https://www.chu.cam.ac.uk/archives/collections/churchill-papers/churchill-biography/. Accessed 22 May 2017.

ccxciii "Sir Winston Churchill: A Chronology." Churchill College, Cambridge. https://www.chu.cam.ac.uk/archives/collections/churchill-papers/churchill-biography/. Accessed 22 May 2017.

ccxciv Soames, Mary. Speaking for Themselves: The Private Letters of Sir Winston and Lady Churchill. 1999.

ccxcv Soames, Mary. Speaking for Themselves: The Private Letters of Sir Winston and Lady Churchill. 1999.

ccxcvi "Sir Winston Churchill: A Chronology." Churchill College, Cambridge. https://www.chu.cam.ac.uk/archives/collections/churchill-papers/churchill-biography/. Accessed 22 May 2017.

ccxcvii "Sir Winston Churchill: A Chronology." Churchill College, Cambridge. https://www.chu.cam.ac.uk/archives/collections/churchill-papers/churchill-biography/. Accessed 22 May 2017.

ccxcviii Soames, Mary. Speaking for Themselves: The Private Letters of Sir Winston and Lady Churchill. 1999.

ccxcix "Sir Winston Churchill: A Chronology." Churchill College, Cambridge. https://www.chu.cam.ac.uk/archives/collections/churchill-papers/churchill-biography/. Accessed 22 May 2017.

ccc Jenkins, Roy. Churchill: A Biography. 2011.

ccci "Sir Winston Churchill: A Chronology." Churchill College, Cambridge. https://www.chu.cam.ac.uk/archives/collections/churchill-papers/churchill-biography/. Accessed 22 May 2017.

cccii Canby, Henry Seidel, and editors. "The 100 Outstanding Books of 1924-1944." Life. August 1944.

ccciii "Sir Winston Churchill: A Chronology." Churchill College, Cambridge. https://www.chu.cam.ac.uk/archives/collections/churchill-papers/churchill-biography/. Accessed 22 May 2017.

ccciv Wainright, Martin. "Winston Churchill's Butterfly House Brought Back to Life." The Guardian. August 2010.

https://www.theguardian.com/environment/2010/aug/19/winston-churchill-butterfly. Accessed 22 May 2017.

cccv "Sir Winston Churchill: A Chronology." Churchill College, Cambridge. https://www.chu.cam.ac.uk/archives/collections/churchill-papers/churchill-biography/. Accessed 22 May 2017.

cccvi Moran, Lord. Winston Churchill: The Struggle for Survival 1940-1965. 1966.

cccvii Churchill, Winston. Painting as a Pastime. 1948

cccviii Pawle, Gerald. The War and Colonel Warden. 1963.

cccix "Leading Churchill Myths: The Myth of the Black God." International Churchill Society. https://www.winstonchurchill.org/publications/finest-hour/finest-hour-155/the-myth-of-the-black-dog. Accessed 27 May 2017.

cccx Abate, Frank R. The Oxford Desk Dictionary of People and Places. 1999. https://books.google.com/books?id=6xxYAgAAQBAJ&pg=PA329#v=onepage&q&f=false. Accessed 20 June 2017.

cccxi "Roosevelt's Genealogy." Franklin D. Roosevelt Presidential Library and Museum. http://www.fdrlibrary.marist.edu/archives/resources/genealogy.html. Accessed 19 June 2017.

cccxii Marrin, Albert. FDR and the American Crisis. 2015.

cccxiii Burns, James MacGregor. Roosevelt. 1956.

cccxiv Burns, James MacGregor. Roosevelt. 1956.

cccxv Burns, James MacGregor. Roosevelt. 1956.

cccxvi Smith, Jean Edward. FDR. 2007.

cccxvii Marrin, Albert. FDR and the American Crisis. 2015.

cccxviii Marrin, Albert. FDR and the American Crisis. 2015.

cccxix Smith, Jean Edward. FDR. 2007.

cccxx Black, Conrad. Franklin Delano Roosevelt: Champion of Freedom. 2005.

cccxxi Marrin, Albert. FDR and the American Crisis. 2015.

cccxxii Marrin, Albert. FDR and the American Crisis. 2015.

cccxxiii Marrin, Albert. FDR and the American Crisis. 2015.

cccxxiv Burns, James MacGregor. Roosevelt. 1956.

cccxxv Marrin, Albert. FDR and the American Crisis. 2015.

cccxxvi Gunther, John. Roosevelt in Retrospect. 1950.

cccxxvii Marrin, Albert. FDR and the American Crisis. 2015.

cccxxviii Smith, Jean Edward. FDR. 2007.

cccxxix Gunther, John. Roosevelt in Retrospect. 1950.

cccxxx Gunther, John. Roosevelt in Retrospect. 1950.

cccxxxi "Family of Wealth Gave Advantages." New York Times. 13 April 1945. http://www.nytimes.com/learning/general/onthisday/bday/0130.html. Accessed 20 June 2017.

cccxxxii Gunther, John. Roosevelt in Retrospect. 1950.

cccxxxiii Marrin, Albert. FDR and the American Crisis. 2015.

cccxxxiv Marrin, Albert. FDR and the American Crisis. 2015.

cccxxxv Burns, James MacGregor. Roosevelt. 1956.

cccxxxvi "Obama Joins List of Seven Presidents with Harvard Degrees." Harvard Gazette. 6 November 2008. http://news.harvard.edu/gazette/story/2008/11/obama-joins-list-of-seven-presidents-with-harvard-degrees/. Accessed 20 June 2017.

cccxxxvii Kelly, Erin. "Presidents Roosevelt Awarded Posthumous J.D.s." Columbia Law School. 25 September 2008. http://www.law.columbia.edu/media_inquiries/news_events/2008/september2008/roosevelt_jds. Accessed 20 June 2017.

ABOUT CAPTIVATING HISTORY

A lot of history books just contain dry facts that will eventually bore the reader. That's why Captivating History was created. Now you can enjoy history books that will mesmerize you. But be careful though, hours can fly by, and before you know it; you're up reading way past bedtime.

Get your first history book for free here:
http://www.captivatinghistory.com/ebook

Make sure to follow us on Twitter: @CaptivHistory and Facebook: www.facebook.com/captivatinghistory so you can get all of our updates!

Made in the USA
Lexington, KY
08 May 2019